Cambridge E

T0276379

Elements in Second Language Acquisition
edited by
Alessandro Benati
American University of Sharjah, UAE
John W. Schwieter
Wilfrid Laurier University

PROFICIENCY PREDICTORS IN SEQUENTIAL BILINGUALS

The Proficiency Puzzle

Lynette Austin
Abilene Christian University

Arturo E. Hernandez
University of Houston

John W. Schwieter
Wilfrid Laurier University

CAMBRIDGE
UNIVERSITY PRESS

CAMBRIDGE
UNIVERSITY PRESS

University Printing House, Cambridge CB2 8BS, United Kingdom

One Liberty Plaza, 20th Floor, New York, NY 10006, USA

477 Williamstown Road, Port Melbourne, VIC 3207, Australia

314–321, 3rd Floor, Plot 3, Splendor Forum, Jasola District Centre,
New Delhi – 110025, India

79 Anson Road, #06–04/06, Singapore 079906

Cambridge University Press is part of the University of Cambridge.

It furthers the University's mission by disseminating knowledge in the pursuit of
education, learning, and research at the highest international levels of excellence.

www.cambridge.org
Information on this title: www.cambridge.org/9781108725248
DOI: 10.1017/9781108641395

First published 2019

A catalogue record for this publication is available from the British Library.

ISBN 978-1-108-72524-8 Paperback
ISBN 978-1-108-64139-5 Online
ISSN 2517-7966 (print)
ISSN 2517-7974 (online)

Proficiency Predictors in Sequential Bilinguals

The Proficiency Puzzle

Elements in Second Language Acquisition

DOI: 10.1017/9781108641395
First published online: April 2019

Lynette Austin
Abilene Christian University

Arturo E. Hernandez
University of Houston

John W. Schwieter
Wilfrid Laurier University

Author for correspondence: Lynette Austin, dla08a@acu.edu

Abstract: This Element provides a synthesis of research on variables deemed to impact bilingual language acquisition and offers an overview of research outcomes from a variety of disciplines. An exploratory study takes into account these variables and examines the language acquisition of adult Spanish-English bilinguals across several domains in their two languages. The results demonstrate that the highly interactive nature of a bilingual's two languages is in line with a holistic view of the dynamic, interdependent nature of bilingualism as described by usage-based theories and dynamic systems theories, and by the conceptualization of bilingualism from a dynamic interactive processing perspective.

Keywords: bilingualism, language proficiency, second language acquisition

ISBNs: 9781108725248 (PB), 9781108641395 (OC)
ISSNs: 2517-7974 (online), 2517-7966 (print)

Contents

1 What Are the Key Concepts?

1.1 Variables Related to Bilingual Language Proficiency

A growing body of research addresses factors that impact first language (L1) and second language (L2) acquisition in sequential bilingual speakers.[1] Wide-ranging questions have emerged from the fields of neuroscience, cognitive and developmental psychology, education, and linguistics, examining key issues and concepts (from each discipline's particular perspective) such as: the neural networks that underlie bilingual language skills; differences in cognitive processes and executive functioning demonstrated by early and late bilinguals; the effects of bilingualism on phonological, morphosyntactic, and lexical-semantic aspects of language; and educational models that further or disadvantage bilingual language functioning for literacy acquisition. Though each discipline frames and tests its questions differently, the puzzle that researchers are attempting to put together generally centers on this piece: What makes bilingual speakers proficient, or not, in each of their languages? Knowledge in this area grows with each study, but findings from different researchers and disciplines at times appear contradictory.

Perhaps the most studied factor in the bilingual language acquisition process is the impact of age of acquisition (AOA) of speakers' languages, a question of special interest when bilingual speakers sequentially acquire an L2 after mastering an L1. Many authors examining levels of bilingual language skill attainment have provided evidence that this factor is a primary predictor for determining "native-like" acquisition of languages (Eubank & Gregg, 1999; Johnson & Newport, 1989; Lahmann, Steinkrauss, & Schmid, 2016; Schmid, 2014; Stevens, 1999; van Boxtel, Bongaerts, & Coppen, 2003; Wartenberger, Heckeren, Abutalabi, Cappa, Villringer, & Perani, 2003; Weber-Fox & Neville, 1996, 1999). According to these studies, younger language learners have an advantage over older learners in terms of the ultimate proficiency level obtained in a given language. This notion, the critical period hypothesis (CPH), is a key, and controversial, consideration in this research: reportedly the existence of critical or sensitive periods for language acquisition (and other areas of cognitive development) implies that there are maturational constraints on skill attainment for languages acquired outside these developmental periods (see Rothman, 2008, for a review; also see Hartshorne, Tenenbaum, & Pinker, 2018, for a recent study in support). However, because native-like attainment

---

[1]　We would like to note that although the topic of simultaneous bilingual language acquisition is related to this subject, we do not specifically address it in this Element. Furthermore, while another growing area of inquiry looks at the effects of the L2 on the L1, this is beyond our scope due to space restrictions.

of L2 skills has been documented in some later L2 learners, other explanations for varied outcomes in L2 ability have been considered (Lahmann et al., 2016). These have included sociological factors, such as educational level and length of residence, and psychological factors, such as motivation. In addition, there is strong evidence for individual variation in L2 learning aptitude, as illustrated in the study conducted by Rimfeld, Dale, and Plomin (2015) involving 6,263 pairs of bilingual twins. The authors posited that such individual differences are genetic in nature.

An alternative view, espoused by Hernandez and Li (2007), has centered on early learning being based on sensorimotor processes, which are readily available to children. Later learning, on the other hand, involves more cognitive processing, which includes areas of the brain involved in higher-level cognition, such as the prefrontal cortex (see Hernandez, Hoffman, & Kotz, 2007; Waldron & Hernandez, 2013, for further discussion). Neuroscience has asked questions and identified effects regarding the neural representations and correlates of bilingual speakers' languages, specifically addressing differences within the brain that appear to be related to early versus later language acquisition (see Vaughn & Hernandez, 2018, for a recent example). The sensorimotor hypothesis has been further developed into a framework, Neurocomputational Emergentism, which conceptualizes development as a series of waves in which brain areas involved in relatively simple cognitive functions become interconnected with each other to take on more complex functions (Hernandez et al., 2019a). Cognitive neuroscientists have evaluated the demands of bilingual language processing and found advantages and disadvantages for bilinguals depending on the task (Schmid & Köpke, 2018a).

Linguists have studied the effects that extent and frequency of L2 use have on the degree of proficiency obtained in that language (Bongaerts, 1999; Flege, Yeni-Komshian, & Liu, 1999; White & Genesee, 1996; Yeni-Komshian, Flege, & Liu, 2000). A later line of inquiry concerns the impact of L1 proficiency on L2 learning. Findings from these studies indicate that a high degree of L1 proficiency positively impacts some aspects of L2 acquisition (Eubank & Gregg, 1999; Flege, Yeni-Komshian, & Liu, 1999; Jiang & Kuehn, 2001). Meanwhile, research on language attrition (or loss of structural aspects of a language) indicates that decreased usage of either language can lead to decreased skills in that language (Bylund, 2009, 2018; Köpke, 2004; Montrul, 1999, 2005). In a review of the literature in this area, Köpke (2004) observed that attrition can occur even when L1 is used to some extent on a daily basis, leading to further questions about whether contact with L2 is also a cause of language attrition. Recent studies in the area provide evidence for a language contact hypothesis (e.g., Kartushina, Frauenfelder, & Golestani, 2016).

   Studies attempting to predict or describe relative levels of linguistic skill in bilinguals' languages often display difficulty in defining and measuring language proficiency. Researchers have evaluated language proficiency subjectively and defined it as the ability to converse in a language, as rated by self or others (Cutler, Mehler, Norris, & Segui, 1989). Other researchers have defined proficiency as grammatical ability, or the capacity to perceive and comprehend different units of language, or the level of naming vocabulary (Johnson & Newport, 1989; Oyama, 1976; Perani et al., 1998; Weber-Fox & Neville, 1996). Inconsistency in the definition of proficiency has limited the generalization of findings.

   A more recent strand of investigation has noted that different systems of language may be differentially impacted by the varying factors known to have a relationship to language acquisition (e.g., AOA, extent of language use, mode of learning). For example, bilingual speakers who learn English at a younger age will likely demonstrate a more native-like accent in English (Köpke, 2004; Wartenberger et al., 2003) and show more native-like response patterns to speech sounds (Archila-Suerte, Zevin, Bunta, & Hernandez, 2012). Conversely, persons from this group (in this case, Spanish-English bilinguals with early exposure to English) may demonstrate errors in L1 verb formation because their level of use and exposure to Spanish has decreased (Anderson, 1999). The notion that different language domains could interact differently with the variables of interest (e.g., AOA) may limit the usefulness of some results in terms of their ability to provide clear evidence for a factor's general impact on language or proficiency (see Lahmann et al., 2016, for a discussion).

   Cummins (1981) proposed a model of language proficiency that differentiates between basic conversational communication skills (those encompassed by grammar, syntax, and pronunciation) and the ability to comprehend and use language for higher-level functioning and reasoning. He postulated that language proficiency is actually a dichotomy of skills, with a distinction being made between basic interpersonal communication skills (BICS) and cognitive/academic language proficiency (CALP). As Cummins (1983) explains it, BICS can be conceived of as the ability to participate in "context-embedded," face-to-face communication such as personal conversations. Conversely, cognitive/academic language proficiency requires the ability to manipulate, use, and understand language in decontextualized settings such as academics. As such, CALP is strongly related to literacy skills (Woodcock & Munoz-Sandoval, 2001); however, CALP emerges from BICS. Utilizing this definition of language proficiency, researchers have developed standardized formal measures of CALP that assess skill level in decontextualized language tasks such as completion of verbal analogies (Woodcock & Munoz-Sandoval, 2001).

Interestingly, the BICS/CALP distinction lines up nicely with the sensorimotor/ cognitive argument put forth by Hernandez and Li (2007).

As can be seen from this brief introduction, current research on the topic of bilingual language development and L2 acquisition supports the notion that there are no simple relationships between the AOA and proficiency in that language, or between language use and language proficiency, or between L1 proficiency and L2 proficiency. The difficulty in measuring or describing these relationships is at least partially due to the fact that there is no simple definition of language proficiency. Another factor that makes investigation of these topics challenging is that other variables such as length of residence or level of education may have as much or more impact on language aspects as the more widely studied variables (DeKeyser, Alfi-Shabtay, & Ravid, 2010) and yet may not be accounted for in the majority of studies. Finally, work looking at genetics found cortical and subcortical dopamine, which is known to play a role in cognitive flexibility, also impacts AOA in the ability to maintain a balanced language proficiency profile in both languages (Vaughn & Hernandez, 2018).

In Sections 2 and 3 of this Element, we provide a focused overview of research considering variables deemed to impact bilingual language acquisition (AOA, language use, and L1 proficiency) and highlight research outcomes from a variety of disciplines, including neuroscience, cognitive psychology, linguistics, and education. With this overview as a backdrop, Section 4 will explore a new avenue of research through an exploratory study which examines the language acquisition of adult Spanish-English bilinguals across a range of domains in their two languages. The study takes into account the primary variables that are known to impact L2 acquisition (AOA and frequency of use) and assesses their impact on bilingual language outcomes likely affected in both languages. The study also incorporates consideration of L1 skills into the L2 proficiency equation (L2 accent and cognitive/academic proficiency). Rather than examining L1 or L2 proficiency independent of the characteristics of the other language, we examine similar aspects of bilingual speakers' two languages and consider the interdependent nature of both languages in light of these variables. In Section 5, we offer a discussion of the study's results and their implications for L2 acquisition, bilingualism, and pedagogy. Our discussion acknowledges that the highly interactive nature of the languages of bilingual speakers is in line with a holistic view of the dynamic, interdependent nature of bilingualism as described by usage-based theories (e.g., Tomasello, 2000) and dynamic systems theories (e.g., de Bot, Lowie, & Verspoor, 2007) and by the conceptualization of bilingual language from a dynamic interactive processing perspective (Hernandez, 2013; Hernandez et al., 2019a; Hernandez, Li, & MacWhinney, 2005; Kohnert, 2004; Kohnert, 2013). The impact of language histories and typologies, a newer area of focus in the exploration of bilingual language acquisition, will also be discussed in connection with the study's findings. Section 6 concludes this Element in which we argue for moving away from a deficiency view of bilingual language skills.

2 What Are the Main Branches of Research?

2.1 Not Two Monolinguals in One Brain

An overview of bilingual research begins logically with a discussion of what is currently understood about the structure and functioning of the bilingual brain. In a seminal article, Grosjean (1989) warned neurolinguists against a monolingual view of bilingualism, affirming that "the bilingual is not two monolinguals in one person!" (p. 3). Grosjean observed in this writing that bilinguals have a "unique and specific *linguistic* [emphasis added] configuration" (p. 3). Ongoing research since has served to extend the concept of the unique configuration of bilinguals to include neurocognitive functioning, as well as encompassing the linguistic and communicative abilities originally considered. For example, in the book *The Bilingual Brain*, Hernandez (2013) states that "two languages live inside one brain almost as two species live in an ecosystem. For the most part they peacefully coexist and often share resources. But they also compete for resources especially when under stress, as occurs when there is brain damage" (p. 12). It is inarguable, then, that bilingual speakers must utilize finite cognitive resources to serve the purposes of storing and communicating information in two (or more) language codes. The question then is: To what extent do languages share geography and resources in the bilingual brain, and to what extent do they compete for available resources?[2]

Francis (2012) described the belief that a complex interdependence of some kind exists between L1 and L2 linguistic knowledge and skills, denoting this interdependence as a set of "cognitive-general competencies" (p. 60). The two language codes emerging from these competencies share cognitive mechanisms, which Baker (2006) has specified as an "integrated source of thought" (p. 170). The elements that comprise this integrated base theoretically include an understanding of how language works, as well as specific linguistic knowledge of the acquired language codes (the extent of the linguistic knowledge depends on the amount of input that the bilingual speaker has had access to in each language). Stemming from this integrated base, knowledge and skills

---

[2] At this point, we affirm that much of the research described within this manuscript applies to multilingual speakers as well as bilingual speakers, but multilingual speakers are another population meriting specific attention.

should transfer in some degree from one language to another, one mechanism to another, and there is evidence that this does occur (Schmid & Köpke, 2018a).

In contrast to the sharing of resources, competition for resources within the bilingual brain must also be considered (Hernandez, 2013). This issue appears to be more of an overt reality in sequential bilinguals (those acquiring an L2 after developing fundamental competency in a first), and it is true that with the onset of L2 use, the amount of L1 utilized must decrease, which can lead to attrition of L1 skills. Schmid and Köpke (2018a) pointed out that L1 now "begins to exist in a state of co-activation with a competing language system" (p. 644), which can result in decreased efficiency, accuracy, and speed of overall language processing. Another outcome of the competition for resources, these authors point out, is that variations in L1 code conventions may be induced by contact with the other language.

2.2 Neural Correlates of Bilingualism

As we consider the behavioral phenomena attributed to bilingualism, what are the neural correlates that underlie bilingual language functioning? A key consideration is whether or not the language neural network differs for the function of processing two languages versus one language. In an early treatment of this subject, Abutalebi and Green (2007) summarize the evidence for the convergence of the neural representations for L1 and L2. Wong, Yin, and O'Brien (2016), in a thorough discussion of the topic, describe the evidence for a "universal language network" (involving the perisylvian language areas of Broca's area (BA44) in the inferior frontal lobe, Wernicke's area (BA22) in the superior posterior temporal lobe, and the connecting arcuate fasciculus). As detailed by Wong et al., speech production also involves the caudate nucleus, the superior frontal gyrus, and the superior longitudinal fascicle, while reading recruits the fusiform gyrus and the angular gyrus. The authors noted that evidence supports similar brain activations in bilingual speakers for L1 and L2 in the domains of reading, listening, and speech production. However, as the article further explained, the likelihood that the general or "universal" language network is similar across and between languages (in a bilingual speaker) does not preclude substantial differences in the way different subnetworks function for language processes.

One significant way in which monolinguals and bilinguals are believed to differ is in the structure of the caudate nucleus, where bilingual gray matter volume is higher (Zou, Ding, Abutalebi, Shu, & Peng, 2012). Wong et al. attributed this difference to the specialized executive function of controlling and switching between languages, utilized only by those speaking more than one language. Stocco, Yamasaki, Natalenko, and Prat (2012) also detailed the role of subcortical structures (specifically the striatum of the basal ganglia circuit) in controlling language switching in bilinguals. That unique function also likely contributes to differences in connectivity between bilinguals and monolinguals in the frontoparietal network (bilinguals having stronger connectivity), which is involved in cognitive control (see also Grady, Luk, Craik, & Bialystok, 2015). Increased brain volume and connectivity appear to be bilingual characteristics as well for phonological, lexical-semantic, and syntactic aspects of language processing.

An important caveat is highlighted at this point: Differences between monolinguals and bilinguals regarding brain structure and function (activation) appear to be modulated by the variables of AOA and degree of language proficiency. Recent studies have found that simultaneous bilinguals perform better than early and late sequential bilingual speakers (and monolinguals) on tests of verbal and nonverbal working memory (WM; Delcenserie & Genesee, 2017). In considering why this might be the case, insight is provided from Wong et al. (2016), who summarized the results of various findings by noting that "generally, the earlier a language is learned and the higher proficiency is attained in L2, the more grey matter intensity and white matter integrity are observed" (p. 13). The challenge then is to disentangle the effects of AOA from those of proficiency.

In a functional magnetic resonance imaging (fMRI) study among Mandarin-English bilinguals, Nichols and Joanisse (2016) found that AOA uniquely predicted the degree to which the "universal language network" was involved in L2 processing for a picture-matching task that controlled for language proficiency levels. They identified evidence of increased bilateral activation of these regions for subjects with later AOAs and noted additional recruitment of right hemisphere areas for this group in L2 versus L1 conditions of the study, specifically in the right parahippocampal gyrus. This effect was identified in later bilinguals with high degrees of proficiency (but not early bilinguals). The authors explained this finding by observing that the right parahippocampal gyrus might be recruited for additional support of semantic retrieval of L2, as semantic retrieval is a function of the left parahippocampal gyrus. They utilized this evidence to support some separation of functional and structural networks in bilinguals, noting that the results of this study indicate more effortful speech processing as AOA increases. This aligns with the findings by Archila-Suerte, Zevin, and Hernandez (2015), who found evidence of an age effect in processing L2 speech sounds. These authors noted greater activation of the right middle frontal gyrus for early bilinguals, while later bilinguals of all proficiency levels showed greater activation in the left inferior frontal lobe. Liu and Cao (2016), in a meta-analysis of imaging studies addressing bilingual activation patterns, also found more divergent activation patterns for late versus early bilinguals, noting more activation in language "coordination areas" (left superior frontal gyrus) (p. 71) in later bilingual groups. In general it appears that early acquisition of two languages results in increased activation of the "universal language network," or the perisylvian language region – Broca's and Wernicke's area – along with the anterior and posterior segments connecting those regions (Catani, Jones, & Ffytche, 2005). Nichols and Joanisse (2016), in summarizing their findings, postulated that AOA modulates "widespread, whole-brain white matter connections" (p. 23). Functioning over a lifetime as a highly proficient bilingual, therefore, has a significant impact on brain architecture and processing abilities (Grant, Dennis, & Li, 2014).

Proficiency level is a confounding variable in studies of age effects on the bilingual brain. Presumably, an individual who has spoken a language longer (one who began speaking the language at an earlier age) will have as an outcome a higher degree of ultimate attainment, or proficiency, and it may be the case that neural convergence in the classic or "universal" language networks only happens when a high level of proficiency is attained (Wong et al., 2016). Furthermore, it appears that there is a "bilingual anterior-to-posterior and subcortical shift (BAPSS)" (Grundy, Anderson, & Bialystok, 2017) as proficiency increases. That is to say that while less proficient bilinguals with poorer language performance rely primarily on the frontal regions for top-down language processing, highly proficient bilinguals recruit more from posterior and subcortical structures, which are engaged for automatic/motor/sensory and perceptual tasks.

The focus of many studies is to attempt to distinguish between age effects and proficiency effects, and these may be easier to tease apart through functional results versus brain imaging. Outcomes of functional studies regarding proficiency effects have presented a mixed view of its impact according to the area of linguistic processing under examination. Taking a big-picture perspective on this issue, Wong et al. (2016) summarize previous work by noting that "while phonology and syntactic knowledge are generally more sensitive to age effects (earlier AoA = less activation), lexical semantics, on the other hand, is more affected by proficiency levels (higher proficiency = more L1-like activation, generally)" (p. 13). This assertion fits in nicely with Hernandez and Li's (2007) sensorimotor hypothesis.

2.3 Cognitive Functioning, Bilingualism, and Linguistic Interdependence

Can information from neuroscience provide underpinning for Cummin's (1981) model of a "common underlying proficiency" (CUP), or linguistic interdependence? Baker (2006) has apparently adopted that perspective by relabeling CUP as a central operating system, indicating that integrated cognitive functioning makes possible the representation of meaning in two (or more) language systems. One class of evidence that would tend to provide support for Cummin's model is that coming from studies in cross-linguistic transfer. Simply defined, cross-linguistic transfer is "the incorporation of elements of one language into another" (Dominguez, 2013, p. 169.) Schmid and Köpke (2018a) asserted that cross-linguistic influence is bidirectional; they note that when another language is brought into an existing language system, the L1 invariably shapes, constrains, and influences the language acquisition process. Over time, though, and subject to external factors such as language use, language aptitude, and motivation, the L2 produces effects (known as "effects of the L2 on the first," or EotSlotF) which have clear impact on the L1. In sequential bilinguals, the following are possible outcomes of L1 impact: L2-induced changes in L1 grammar; "borrowing" of elements from the L2 lexicon when using L1; "convergence," or the use of a new system which is neither L1 nor L2; "restructuring" of L1 based on L2; and "attrition" (decrease or loss of the ability to generate utterances in L1) (Dominguez, p. 169).

The functional aspects of cross-linguistic influence, when viewed as language competition, are sometimes described as a "bilingual disadvantage"; Schmid and Köpke (2018a) summarized studies describing an advantage for monolinguals over bilinguals in the latency of lexical retrieval. On the other hand, current research appears to point toward stronger executive functioning among bilinguals, probably due to noted differences in connectivity and in the frontoparietal network (Wong et al., 2016). An earlier meta-analysis of 63 studies addressing the connection between cognitive functions and bilingualism found evidence that increased attentional control, WM, metalinguistic awareness, and abstract and symbolic representation skills are associated with bilingual versus monolingual status (Adesope et al., 2010). It must be noted, however, that a later meta-analysis (Donnelly et al., 2015) of 73 comparisons looking specifically at the cognitive capacity to resolve incongruencies in conflict resolution tasks did *not* find conclusive evidence for a clear bilingual advantage (due primarily to methodological issues in the studies included). Therefore, the question of a bilingual advantage in cognition is an open one.

Despite evidence from some studies for a likely bilingual advantage in cognition, a number of authors view transfer effects from L1 to L2 as generally negative, and the terminology that surrounds the concept of language transfer tends to paint a picture of language erosion, particularly in reference to L2 effects on L1. However, the field of bilingual education tends toward another view – that of positive transfer. From this perspective, L1 is seen as a facilitating structure; an "established and organized system of meaning that can be applied to new learning situations . . . In other words, an individual can use concepts that are already well developed in their primary language to facilitate learning and problem-solving in their L2" (Bylund, 2011, p. 6). This Vygotskian perspective, as Bylund continued to explain, focuses on the intersection between thought and language, recognizing that the capacity to transfer information from L1 is a principal resource for the L2 acquirer. Accordingly, this is available to the learner because significant interdependence exists between the L1 and L2 knowledge and skills. However, this idea, original to Cummin's model, appears to be addressing the transfer of well-developed concepts, described by Vygotsky as "verbal thought," rather than superficial aspects of L1 and L2 language codes, which may differ significantly in external characteristics.

There is discussion in the literature regarding how transfer of external language characteristics indeed occurs between L1 and L2. Francis (2012) suggested that recognition of language elements such as word forms that are or appear to be cognates and awareness of similarities and differences between L1 and L2 word-order patterns, phonological patterns, and morphological forms could be considered as direct transfers from one language code to the other. Francis denoted this interaction as a "mutual influence" (p. 60) and noted further that "such interlinguistic transfers do not have to result in target language forms or native-speaker-like accuracy in production to be useful for the L2 learner."

One language modality which has been utilized to exemplify the "central operating system" function of the bilingual brain is that of reading/literacy. Ganan, Hauser, and Thomas (2015) studied the correlation between Spanish fluency and English reading abilities in a sample of sequential-bilingual second and third graders in bilingual classrooms and found that Spanish oral language fluency was a moderate predictor of English reading comprehension abilities. Outcomes differentiated between students with high proficiency in Spanish versus those with lower proficiency. Proficient speakers were five times more likely to meet criterion on the test of English reading comprehension. For our purposes here, this may be understood considering that when students' L1 skills receive support in academic settings that lead to high levels of L1 proficiency, their information-processing abilities advance farther and faster. Instruction in the L1 along with opportunities to hear and use the L2, as opposed to L2-only instruction, permits the development of "academic language skills," including metacognitive and metalinguistic abilities needed for literacy development. Otherwise, as Francis (2012) points out, if content instruction is provided only in the L2, the result may be "delayed or abated learning of higher-order academic proficiencies (p. 73)." Earlier studies provide support for these findings; most notably Ramirez, Yuen, and Ramey's (1991) quasi-experimental study, including over 2,000 participants, which looked at ultimate L2 reading attainment in bilingual children being educated in L2 or L1, found that students receiving L1 support in educational programming demonstrated stronger L2 literacy outcomes.

To bring the discussion back to insights from neuroscience that would support the notion of linguistic interdependence in bilingual speakers, it appears the strengths in executive functioning noted in bilinguals might translate into stronger metalinguistic and metacognitive skills, which are considered aspects of the CUP. This is explained by Wong et al. (2016), who noted that cognitive control mechanisms support metalinguistic skills such as phonological and morphological awareness, and this is where a bilingual advantage is seen.

2.4 A Bilingual "Disadvantage"? Language-Specific Skills in Bilinguals

Although the conceptual knowledge and metalinguistic skills which appear to transfer between a bilingual's languages can be considered a bilingual advantage, there does appear to be a bilingual disadvantage when language skills specific to each language are considered. For example, lexical representation and verbal fluency appear stronger in monolinguals than in bilinguals working in either language; for bilinguals, this is manifested as a deficit in language-specific vocabulary knowledge (Wong et al., 2016). The indication that bilinguals have fewer vocabulary exemplars in each of their languages is not surprising due to the fact that vocabulary is to some degree distributed across the two languages; however, the implication that language processing is more effortful for bilingual speakers does appear as a "disadvantage." One way of viewing this disadvantage is to understand that (likely due to differences in external variables such as use, length of residence, motivation, and others) the performance of bilinguals in language-specific skills at a supposed end state of language development is less consistent than that of mature monolingual speakers (Schmid & Köpke, 2018a).

With this overview in mind of converging and conflicting information about bilingual language acquisition and the effects of two languages in one brain, the remainder of this Element will examine evidence regarding the major predictors of AOA, amount of language use, and degree of L1 proficiency on specific bilingual language outcomes. That exploration will then provide the foundation for an exploratory study testing some of those predicted outcomes.

3 What Are the Key Readings?

3.1 Age of L2 Acquisition and Learning

3.1.1 Primary Questions Regarding L2 Acquisition

Questions regarding developmental and educational aspects of bilingualism have been addressed through studies that consider variables from individuals' language backgrounds as predictors of a number of language and academic outcomes. Research questions often have emerged from practical concerns, many centered on whether better outcomes (e.g., in education) occur in an L2 if that language is introduced at an earlier age. This is particularly true of research on bilingualism in the United States, where educational legislation would indicate that a significant priority for child bilingual speakers is the eventual level of English language (majority language) proficiency attained, with expected resulting academic achievement (Baca & Cervantes, 1998).

Answers to the question regarding the impact of AOA have varied according to which aspect of language is being examined (e.g., grammar versus accent versus phonological awareness skills). As questions relating to AOA have been studied, other variables of interest have surfaced. These have included the impact of amount of language use on language outcomes. Another area of focus is the degree to which L1 is developed, prior to or as L2 is acquired. Within this focus, questions regarding the impact of amount of contact time with L1 have arisen, addressing both quality and quantity of input in each language (Köpke, 2004).

In reviewing the literature that describes the predictor variables that have been addressed in studies of bilingualism, it is timely to take a bilingual view of the language skills outcomes typically investigated. As researchers explore the complex of variables associated with bilingual language acquisition (primarily AOA, amount of language use, and cognitive/academic language proficiency), is it possible to predict a profile of specific bilingual language skills based on those variables?

An application of this sort of research might be found in the arena of language assessment. It is noted that many current assessments utilized for developmental or academic assessment of language skills focus on "monolingual" expectations for language outcomes. For example, one popular developmental assessment of Spanish language skills tests young children on their mastery of advanced verb forms. However, there is some indication in the literature that these forms may drop out of usage for some Spanish-English bilingual speakers (Anderson, 1999, 2001). Could an understanding of the impact of different variables on bilingual language skills enable examiners to identify speakers for which monolingual normative expectations would likely be inappropriate? Related questions of interest arise; for example, although accent may be more "native-like" in L2 if it is introduced at an earlier age, does it follow that cognitive and academic language proficiency outcomes are similarly impacted? Are the different skills represented by outcomes in phonological discrimination/production, and advanced semantic knowledge, for example, equally affected by early acquisition of L2?

3.1.2 How Important Is Age of Acquisition?

Popular understanding of bilingualism indicates that only very young learners acquire an L2 to a native-like level of proficiency. This topic has been of interest to the general public for many years and continues to appear in periodicals and newspapers; for example, the May 28, 2018, edition of *Time* contains a health column entitled "Why kids learn languages more easily than you do" (Ducharme, 2018). Observers see that whereas children normally learn language easily and successfully, adults learning an L2 show significant variability in outcomes (Rothman, 2008), and this intuitively leads to the conclusion that young learners are biologically equipped for language learning, whereas adults are not.

This interest in L2 AOA is reflected in the scholarly literature, where the impact of AOA on the development of an individual's proficiency in speaking an L2 has been a primary topic in the field. In the literature addressing questions of age and bilingualism, the variable AOA has been operationalized in at least two different ways. One is the age of arrival to a new country (for immigrant populations) (Stevens, 1999), and the other is the age of significant exposure to a new language (or the point at which systematic learning of the language begins) (Bialystok & Miller, 1999; Kohnert, 2004; Weber-Fox & Neville, 1996) (for both immigrant and native-born bilinguals).

Implied in the notion that AOA matters in L2 acquisition is the idea that acquisition of an L2 may be subject to maturational constraints. This assumption is controversial (Nikolov, 2009). As Silverberg and Samuel (2004) point out, experimenters cannot manipulate the age of L2 acquisition in research participants. As a result, this variable is essentially a correlational one and may be subject to covariance with many factors, such as the extent of language use, individual cognitive abilities, and the conditions under which the L2 is acquired. Some studies have supported the notion that these other sociological or psychological/cognitive factors may better account for differential outcomes in L2 acquisition than AOA; Lahmann et al. (2016) summarize research reporting varied outcomes on linguistic behavioral tests in discussing this controversy. The authors report robust age effects for grammatical proficiency and a lack of age effects for lexical/vocabulary acquisition in L2, for example. In discussing these outcomes, the authors note a confound, observed by several others, in the research: A number of studies addressing grammatical attainment do note that at times older L2 learners acquire "native-like" grammatical abilities in L2, which would contradict the supposition that age is the primary factor influencing L2 attainment.

Although studies' results may vary as to what aspects of language behavior are or are not impacted by AOA or to what extent language is affected by this variable, the convergence of evidence indicates that there are clear differences in the processing of L2 as a function of AOA (Silverberg & Samuel, 2004). These functional and structural variations related to AOA will be discussed at greater length later in this writing, but the relevant question at this point is: How should these differences be interpreted? Why does age matter in L2 acquisition?

3.1.3 Age of Acquisition and the Critical Period Hypothesis for L2 Acquisition

One proposed answer is found in the CPH, as applied to L2 acquisition. In brief, the CPH states that there is a limited developmental period, or window of opportunity, during which it is physiologically possible for individuals to acquire a language to normal levels of proficiency in an L1 (Birdsong, 1999). In other words, AOA is important in L2 learning because older learners encounter physiological constraints to L2 learning which very young learners (those within the critical period) do not. If, as many hypothesize, the CPH for L2 acquisition (CPH-L2A) is connected to physiological changes in the brain (i.e., loss of brain cell plasticity) specific to language that take place before puberty, specifically prior to age 15 (Johnson & Newport, 1989), then learners who begin to acquire a language after the onset of puberty should be unable to reach a native-like level of attainment in that language (van Boxtel, Bongaerts, & Coppen, 2003). Nikolov (2009) succinctly summarizes the assumptions of the CPH-L2A: "the CPH claims that natural language acquisition is available to young children, whereas older adolescents and adults have limited or no access to it" (p. 4).

An assumption relevant to the application of the CPH-L2A is that L2 proficiency should show a discontinuous function across AOAs (Bialystok & Miller, 1999). This would mean that in studies examining the impact of AOA, there *should* be an effect for early learning of a language, but that age of L2 learning should cease to matter beyond that early stage – when subjects have an AOA that is beyond the critical period. However, a significant number of studies in areas where an age effect has been advanced show a *continuous* negative correlation between AOA and attainment (such as in the area of L2 grammar acquisition), suggesting that the factor(s) at work here may be other confounding variables such as "L1 development and use, typological distance between the L1 and the L2, [or] learners' motivation and attitude" as well as "length of residence and level of education" (Lahmann et al., 2016, p. 359–60). Silvina Montrul is one of the frequently cited authors who finds that there are significant limitations to the evidence for a strong CPH, stating that much of the available literature does not support it (see Montrul, Davidson, De La Fuente, & Foote, 2014).

In refuting authors who utilize the continuous versus discontinuous decline argument in discrediting or at least de-emphasizing the CPH-L2A hypothesis, Long (2013) argued convincingly for a "sensitive period" (SP) in L2 learning, noting that evidence for such is ample (p. 9). He described the SP in L2 acquisition as a period of "residual plasticity" that persists beyond the critical, or most sensitive, developmental periods connected to L1 acquisition. Oyama (1976) first raised this possibility in considering the pattern of decline of later L2 learner outcomes in phonology, and Long expanded on her and others' arguments as follows: There can be significant individual variability in L2 acquisition, in part attributed to language aptitude and learning environment; the fact that this variability is present does not mean that AOA is not a primary factor in the process. The SP hypothesis connects to a variety of studies examining linguistic behavioral outcomes. There is evidence in these for qualitative changes in the rate of decline (as the SP hypothesis does not demand the sharp rate of decline necessary to support a strict CPH-L2A view). Outcomes in areas such as grammatical judgment tests, oral and written grammatical production measures, phonology, and even some lexical outcomes (specifically in the areas of idiom acquisition) provide evidence for this conclusion (Long provided a comprehensive review of these). Finally, Long reiterated, in discussing these qualitative skill changes, an earlier notion that the SPs for different language skills vary, and that this may contribute to the confusion/lack of consensus on the topic of critical periods for L2 learning (see Long, 2013, for discussion).

Given the controversy circling the CPH-L2A (at least from a linguistic behavior stance), some scholars question the utility of the construct. Rothman (2008) noted that implicit in questions connected to the CPH-L2A is the idea that adults don't learn in the same way as children. He reflected that in considering the CPH for L2 application, researchers are really considering domain-general, or implicit, learning (versus domain-specific, or explicit, learning). Rothman circled back to question whether or not critical/sensitive periods in L2 learning can even be considered when the products being assessed as evidence for or against these phenomena are evaluated within adult learners who had a normal L1 development. However, as will be seen later in this Element, studies in neuroscience provide a different perspective.

A second, strong counterclaim to the hypothesis of CPH-L2A is the observation, made by a number of authors, that late L2 acquirers with native-like proficiency in L2 exist. Their existence would appear to contradict the CPH-L2A claim that biology imposes maturational constraints on L2 acquisition (Lahmann et al., 2016; Montrul et al., 2014; Nikolv, 2009.) However, some proponents of the CPH-L2A utilize the "domain-general versus domain-specific learning" argument to explain such cases. These authors note that older learners have access to compensatory mechanisms, such as conscious declarative memory, metalinguistic skills, and pragmatic abilities, to counter the decline in implicit language-learning competence which they believe to be inevitable (Nikolov, 2009).

One could easily criticize all these views for the focus on the outcome of language learning without considering how language learning occurs. As noted earlier, Hernandez and Li (2007) proposed that as children grow older they transition from sensorimotor to cognitive processing. However, even this view does not describe the mechanism or mechanisms that are involved in how the system evolves over time. Critical period work usually suggests waves of plasticity that gradually become restricted over time (Werker & Hensch, 2015). Thus, considerable work remains in order to understand the multidimensional and dynamic nature of how a human interacts with the world and which ways this interaction leads to gradual reduction in the ability to learn an L2.

In summary, the evidence from behavioral studies of specific language skills does support the notion that there are age effects for L2 acquisition. The finding that "child starters outperform adult starters [in L2] in the long run" presented in the seminal paper on this subject (Krashen, Long, & Scarcella, 1979, as cited by Nikolov, 2009, p. 4) has been confirmed by most studies since then. Those building and refining theoretical frameworks for L2 acquisition contend for or refute the theory that critical/sensitive periods are the source for these age effects, and the discussion continues. This Element will revisit the CPH-L2A debate as viewed by the discipline of cognitive neuroscience, but first we continue the discussion of language behaviors in bilingual speakers by examining the effects that L2 acquisition has on L1 competence.

3.2 Age of L2 Acquisition and L1 Attrition

Just as the L2 AOA can be viewed as an intervening variable in the eventual level of L2 proficiency achieved, it may also be an intervening variable in the level of L1 proficiency demonstrated by the adult bilingual speaker. Montrul (2005) made the claim that when L2 is learned early in childhood (prior to the age of 5) the L1 grammar at adulthood may be incomplete, similar to the L2 grammar of an intermediate speaker. Montrul noted that this phenomenon, known as L1 loss, is basically the reciprocal of L2 gain. She explained that the term "language loss" is a general term used to refer both to attrition, seen in older L2 learners, and to incomplete acquisition, which may occur in early bilinguals.

Bylund (2018) described the language products of this phenomenon as "forms that diverge from native, monolingual behavior" (p. 683). These divergent language forms are evidence of "attrition" when changes in the language environment which are presumed to cause language changes occur in teen years or later. Bylund also referred to the term "heritage language acquisition" as the equivalent of the incomplete acquisition which Montrul (2005) references. In further discussion, Bylund highlighted the difficulty in determining at what point "incomplete acquisition/heritage language acquisition" can be identified, in that the so-called divergent language forms which are considered indicative of incomplete acquisition could also simply be forms that have not yet been mastered. Such difficulties notwithstanding, comprehensive consideration of the effects of age on bilingual language acquisition must consider the variations, or so-termed deviations, in grammar, lexicon, and phonology that are often manifested in the L1 of the speaker (Bylund, 2009).

Anderson (1999, 2004) synthesized the results of several studies and identified four main patterns of L1 grammatical variation that have been attributed to language loss or incomplete acquisition: (1) reduction of inflectional morphology and correspondingly less flexible word order; (2) regularization of irregular patterns; (3) decreased use of coordinated sentences and embedded clauses, and (4) transfer of L2 syntactic structure to L1. She observed a number of these characteristics in the language of a typically developing Spanish-English speaking bilingual child, whose language use she described in a case study. The child learned Spanish and English from birth. Errors in Spanish were observed in verb inflections (particularly with the later developing subjunctive mood), noun phrase agreement (gender agreement), and syntax. Anderson noted that the child appeared to have an incomplete acquisition of Spanish grammar, when compared to monolingual Spanish-speaking children her age. Although such attrition is not unusual, range of proficiency in L1 varies widely, with some early and late bilinguals demonstrating high levels of proficiency as native speakers while others have limited productive ability (Montrul, 2005).

Attrition has a much greater impact on the L1 language skills of young bilingual speakers than on those of later L2 acquirers, which suggests a maturational effect (Bylund, 2009; Köpke & Schmid, 2003). When language loss occurs, children's language systems attrite more extensively across language domains (pronunciation, grammatical knowledge), and attrition occurs more rapidly in younger speakers. Dominguez (2013) cited a number of studies supporting this observation, noting that changes in the language skills of young bilingual speakers tend to be more dramatic and substantial, whereas the attrition shown by later bilinguals does not show the same degree of significant grammatical change. Dominguez also referenced the evidence for greater individual variation in the changes experienced by later bilinguals. Specific to this group of speakers, emotional, attitudinal, and motivational factors have also been theorized to play roles in individual variation in attrition (Köpke, 2003).

Bylund (2009) observed that age 12 seems to be around the time when susceptibility to attrition is decreased in contexts where reduced language contact is judged to be the cause of attrition. Bylund noted that in speakers with ages of reduced contact (ARC) of five or younger, attrition is more significant than with speakers with ARC of 10 or above; in other words, susceptibility to attrition is not equally high up to the age of 12 but rather shows a gradual decrease across childhood. Interestingly, the impact of age on attrition may be noted particularly in the ease with which an attriter regains language skills with reactivation of language use; individuals with attrited skills who have later ARCs are more likely to regain L1 features with training or immersion (Bylund, 2009). Thus, studies in both areas (those looking at skills lost by different ARC groups and those looking at skills regained via L1 reactivation by different ARC groups) can be said to support maturational effects on L1 attrition.

One group which has been heavily studied along these lines is the group of international adoptees. Pallier et al. (2003) provided a striking example of attrition in young language learners in a study of the L1 skills of young international adoptees (adopted before age eight). As adults, these individuals demonstrated no remaining L1 proficiency years after having been removed from the L1 environment. Bylund (2009) referred to this and other studies having similar outcomes, which researchers came to view as representing "neural resetting" (p. 702). Ventureyra, Pallier, and Yoo (2004), for example, suggested a possible explanation for the lack of effect that early exposure to L1 had on L1 phonology in adult adoptees who had lost L1 skills. They noted that "the effects of AOA before the age of 10 are not due to an irreversible decrease of neural plasticity with age but are rather due to an increased stabilization of the neural network by the learning of L1. When exposure to L1 ceases, then the network could somehow 'reset' and L2 would be acquired fully" (p. 89). In these cases, L1 reactivation studies could potentially support an age effect in cases of such severe attrition, and indeed, Bylund (2009) cited a few studies where an "abandoned" language was reactivated through training and noted that the degree to which the "L1 remnants" may be reactivated appears related to ARC (p. 691). With respect to language phonological features, Bylund suggested that these studies indicate that early language exposure has long-term effects, regardless of the level at which the language in question is maintained.

3.3 Age of L2 Acquisition and Cognitive/Cortical Effects in Bilinguals

3.3.1 Evidence from Neurophysiological Research

As previously referenced, the fields of cognitive neuroscience and psychology have advanced research that supports the CPH-L2A. In a seminal study, Weber-Fox and Neville (1996) found evidence from event-related brain potentials (ERPs) indicating that "maturational changes significantly constrain the development of the neural systems that are relevant for language" (p. 231). According to their results, ERP latencies (when compared to those of native speakers) were affected by delays in L2 exposure as short as 1–3 years (L2 exposure occurring after the first birthday) in the area of syntactic skills. In the area of semantic skills greater ERP latencies were observed for those exposed to English (L2) after age 11 and after age 16. No significant differences in ERP latencies for the semantic task were identified for individuals acquiring L2 at any point prior to age 11.

In subsequent studies, imaging processes became a more viable option for addressing the question of what effects varying AOAs may have on cortical representation of language. Initial fMRI studies reported conflicting results in terms of the impact of AOA on cortical representation of language with some studies failing to support a correlation (Chee, Tan, & Thiel, 1999; Kim, Relkin, Lee, & Hirsch, 1997). It became clear that researchers had to address the confound of language proficiency in evaluating whether differences in L1 and L2 processing were potentially due to age effects; in other words, utilizing L2 speakers of varying proficiency levels placed varying cortical processing demands on those speakers and obscured potential effects due to AOA. Perani et al. (1998), for example, found that when proficiency was kept constant, AOA did not appear to have an impact on the brain's representation of L2 when the task involved listening to (and by extension comprehending) stories in the L2 for individuals learning a language before age four versus learning it after age 10. Other researchers observed a similar modulating effect for proficiency in examining the role of age: for lexical/semantic skills, a number of studies measuring latency of responses (Hernandez, Bates & Avila, 1996; Hernandez & Kohnert, 1999; Hernandez & Reyes, 2002) found that proficiency rather than AOA was significant in determining latency of response, with more proficient speakers demonstrating faster naming.

Weber-Fox and Neville (1999) later agreed that "converging evidence... suggests that specialized systems that mediate different aspects of language may be distinct in their susceptibilities to alterations in the timing of L2 learning" (p. 35). They continued to emphasize that results from behavioral and imaging studies support the contention that AOA is the best predictor for ultimate language skill attainment. In an fMRI study, Wartenberger et al. (2003) did identify differences between AOA groups based on the type of language skills assessed. When considering effects of age and level of proficiency in the L2, they found that AOA affected the cortical representation of grammatical processes in L2 (with the late acquisition/highly proficient group showing bilateral activation in the inferior frontal gyrus (Brodmann area [BA] 44 and 44/6), and the early acquisition/high proficiency group showing activation only in the left hemisphere). Conversely, semantic skills appeared to be mainly impacted by the speakers' proficiency levels in the L2, with no activation differences based on AOA.

Newman et al. (2012) returned to study brain activation in bilingual speakers using ERPs, while controlling for L1 and L2 proficiency levels. The authors studied participants' ERP responses to lexical/semantic violations in sentences, while treating proficiency in each language as a continuous variable versus the typical categorical variable treatment (high proficiency/low proficiency). Using this model, they found that *no* residual variance from the ERP data outside of variance predicted by proficiency could be attributed to group status (of native or later language learner), failing to support age effects for L2 acquisition in the language area of semantics (in line with other studies). On the other hand, in another ERP-based study, Pakulak and Neville (2011) found an age effect for syntactic processing when they compared matched-proficiency groups of native versus non-native English speakers. In their discussion, they suggest that late L2 learners with high L2 proficiency rely on different neural mechanisms than do early or native speakers of a language.

Accordingly, imaging studies of the neuroanatomical structures underlying bilingualism continue to provide evidence in support of the CPH-L2A.

In Nichols and Joanisse's (2016) fMRI study mentioned earlier, there were significant activation differences between different AOA groups matched for language proficiency, which the authors associated with "distinct types of plasticity for age-dependent effects" (p. 21) versus experience and proficiency effects. This conclusion is in line with the findings and discussion of Wei and colleagues (2015), who make a case for the "reworking" of the human brain when in contact with more than one language. These authors conducted fine-grained morphometry analyses of bilingual participants' fMRI scans and found that earlier L2 exposure was associated with larger volumes in the right parietal cortex (angular gyrus and superior parietal lobe), specifically that the right SPL increased as AOA decreased. For these age-based comparisons, the data were controlled for proficiency and language exposure factors. Notably, while the authors did find effects (to be discussed later) for those variables as well, in the hierarchical multiple regression analysis, AOA explained 21% of the variance of the dependent variables. Proficiency and current language exposure predicted only 10% and 1% of the variance, respectively.

Interestingly, a significant difference was found between early and late bilinguals' brain activation during L1 processing in the meta-analysis of imaging studies conducted by Liu and Cao (2016). The left fusiform gyrus (BA 37) was found to be more activated in early bilinguals than late bilinguals during L1 processing when task type and level of L2 proficiency were matched. No region was observed to be more activated for late bilinguals than early bilinguals during L1 processing. The authors identified these findings as "initial evidences that L2 AOA influences the L1 brain network" (p. 66).

In summarizing the data from neuroscience, age effects attributable to the CPH-L2A appear to be solidly supported by a variety of data. Neuroimaging data consistently show structural variation secondary to AOA groupings. Interestingly, neurophysiological data such as ERPs show age effects for syntactic and phonological processes but not for semantic processes.

3.3.2 Evidence from Cognitive Research

From a cognitive psychology perspective, theorists have discussed the overall significance of underlying cognitive abilities for all types of learned behaviors (Elman, 1993). Following up, Eubank and Gregg (1999) noted that there are various mental faculties that may be related to linguistic competence (i.e., short-term memory, episodic memory, auditory perception) and that other aspects of linguistic competence are autonomous from these abilities. Suggesting that language itself is an "epiphenomenon," or a gross categorization of the working together of these various abilities, they promoted the idea that there are multiple critical periods for all of the different competencies. Köpke (2004) further developed this notion by citing arguments which link L2 acquisition to the learner's previous linguistic knowledge base and cognitive ability/cognitive maturity. From this perspective, age-related differences might be considered to have both positive and negative effects on L2 learning. For example, procedural or implicit memory may be the system which serves L1 acquisition, and implicit memory is known to be less accessible to older individuals; on the other hand, older learners are more skilled at applying explicit, declarative memory for language learning (Paradis, 1994). Other researchers have developed the procedural-implicit memory versus the explicit-declarative memory model in exploring age differences in L2 learning and connected an apparent age effect in favor of younger learners for morphosyntactic processing tasks. These are deemed to recruit procedural-implicit memory. Wong and colleagues (2016) provide an updated discussion of this hypothesis.

In a related paper, van Boxtel et al. (2003) supported the notion that younger L2 learners have an advantage over older learners in L2 acquisition due to initial WM limitations. Children process smaller units of information than adults do and, therefore, perhaps focus more intently on details such as grammatical forms. Adults may tend not to notice these as they attempt to process larger units of information. Based on this perspective, the age-related factor that governs this difference between children and adults may not be specific to language. Connecting this notion to bilingualism, differences on traditional tasks involving verbal short-term memory (STM) and WM, as well as nonverbal WM, were associated with the age of L2 acquisition in a study by Delcenserie and Genesee (2017). The study controlled for variables of proficiency and overall cognitive ability. Simultaneous bilinguals demonstrated an advantage over early (AOA of 4–6 years of age) and later (AOA of 7–15 years) language learners. No difference was found in STM and WM abilities between the early and later successive bilingual groups, which may be interpreted as providing evidence for the CPH relevant to these abilities.

A recent meta-analysis by Grundy and Timmer (2017) also pointed to likely age effects for a bilingual advantage in WM. In a review of 88 effect sizes in 27 independent studies, the authors identified a "significant small to medium population effect size of 0.20 in favor of greater working memory capacity for bilinguals than monolinguals" (p. 325). Moderator analyses indicated that children demonstrated the largest effects over other age groups.

In a newer approach to explaining cognitive functioning related to language use in simultaneous versus sequential bilinguals, Vaughn and Hernandez (2018) explored intergroup differences between persons with different genotypes. The genotype groups associated with higher levels of subcortical dopamine appeared to show an age-advantage for L2 learning that the researchers connected to procedural (motor) learning-based processes (i.e., those recruiting implicit memory). On the other hand, later AOAs appeared to be better for individuals from genotypes that were associated with higher levels of dopamine in the prefrontal cortex, where learning is based on executive attention and WM processes. This suggests that the CPH-L2A may only be true for certain (groups of) individuals.

Perceptual abilities have also been posited as underlying language-learning skills and believed to be impacted by critical periods. The perception and processing of L2 speech sounds in bilinguals have been shown in some studies to demonstrate an AOA effect, with some denoting the phonological system as being the language system most impacted by age effects (Wong et al., 2016). Early bilingual acquirers demonstrate greater brain activation in prefrontal regions when processing L2 speech sounds, implicating WM involvement, whereas later bilinguals and monolinguals show greater engagement for perceptual processing in the expected temporal lobe regions (STG) (Archila-Suerte et al., 2015). Interestingly, vowel perception may differ from consonant processing in this regard; Flege and MacKay (2004) did not find a strong advantage for early (pre-adolescent) L2 learning for auditory perception of vowels, noting that although later L2 learners were generally less adept at perceiving English vowels, some perceived them accurately.

3.3.3 Other Influencing Factors

It is important to note that motivation plays a strong role in cognitive control of learning processes. Stevens (1999) observed that L2 learning is prompted by opportunities and motivations to become proficient. In considering English proficiency for bilingual speakers in the United States, length of residence in the United States (which links with AOA) strongly predicts English proficiency, for example, as does educational attainment. Very young learners, starting before the age of five, were almost certain to report proficient use of L2 in adulthood. In Steven's study, this effect was mediated by the previously mentioned factors (education, residence) as well as by activity characteristics such as whether or not the subjects were in the labor force or enrolled in school. Another predictor of L2 proficiency was whether or not the subjects had spouses and/or children fluent in L2. Stevens noted that the large variance observed in proficiency levels among later immigrants is congruent with the notion that fluency is more likely to develop in settings that encourage English learning.

Bialystok and Hakuta (1999) described social factors that may facilitate L2 learning for younger as opposed to older learners. For example, younger learners are more likely to be exposed to nurturing environments such as school and provided with simplified L2 input. Finally, they are more likely to have cooperative peers involved as they acquire L2, a significant motivational factor.

In a more recent review of internal factors influencing L2 learning, Zafar (2012) highlighted these variables as areas demonstrating significant individual differences in language learners: age, sex, aptitude, motivation, learning styles, learning strategies, personality. Zafar's summary of the literature touching on each variable indicated that the research on these individual differences had not advanced to the point where a coherent theory or theories can be advanced. Zafar suggested that "the growing awareness of the need to focus on the individual ... will fuel the need to study the phenomenon in a detailed and empirical manner" (p. 644). Ardasheva's (2016) study of 805 young (3rd–8th grade) ESL learners identified these significant contributors to English language outcomes for these learners: metacognitive strategies, motivation, and native language literacy. These outcomes appear to be significant pedagogically for sequential bilingual learners acquiring L2 in an academic setting.

3.4 Language Use and Linguistic, Cognitive, and Cortical Effects

Frequency of language (L2) use is a significant variable in predicting L2 proficiency. In fact, it may be argued that language use appears to be just as significant as AOA in impacting L2 acquisition. A number of studies have indicated that if a learner has continued access to (and implied opportunities to use) the L2, and it is important to him to learn the L2, then there is a possibility the learner will attain native-like levels of L2 proficiency. Bongaerts (1999) drew this conclusion in an early study on the topic focusing on proficiency in L2 pronunciation, and White and Genesee (1996) reported similar results in the area of grammar for late L2 learners. Flege et al. (1999) conducted another study of English grammar abilities with L2 learners and reported that the variables most salient in grammaticality judgment were number of years of schooling in the United States and the amount of English use by the bilinguals.

Later studies have sought, among other things, to distinguish between the roles of exposure and expression, under the broad topic of the impact of "language use." Hammer, Komaroff, Rodriguez, Lopez, Scarpino, and Goldstein (2012), in a study of predictors of the bilingual language skills of 448 Latino children, found that the quantity of (receptive) exposure that the children received played a somewhat different role than the quantity of (expressive) use that the children demonstrated in their languages. Exposure was a primary predictor of L1 (Spanish) semantic skills, whereas use (expression) predicted L2 (English) semantic abilities to a greater degree.

Bylund (2009) elaborated on the role of language use and other factors in L2 acquisition, signaling maturation as the primary influencer before puberty (with an inverse relation between age and degree of proficiency attained). Nonbiological factors take over after puberty, including language use and sociopsychological factors (such as generational status, parental variables, motivation, and individual aptitude). He suggested these nonbiological factors may provide a counterbalance to the impact of maturational factors in both L2 learning and L1 attrition – in other words, language exposure/use play different roles in the process with an older bilingual speaker, for both languages.

3.4.1 Language Use and L2 Learning

Proficiency in L2 pronunciation, usually focused on degree of perceived accent, is a particularly productive area of research addressing the impact of language use. Flege (1999) admitted that earlier appears to be better as far as L2 pronunciation is concerned; however, he related this phenomenon to the effect of the previously developed L1 phonetic system and the interaction between it and L2. He also identified a difference in L2 accent (less accent) as a function of the amount of L1 use. In a later study, Yeni-Komshian et al. (2000) found that in a sample of Korean-English bilinguals, only 49% demonstrated native-like pronunciation of the L1, Korean. Most of the subjects with "native-like" pronunciation were late L2 (English) learners; the early L2 learners were less likely to accurately pronounce Korean phonemes. In this study, the group that attained above-average proficiency in L1 and L2 pronunciation demonstrated frequent use of both languages.

A similar effect has been seen for semantic and syntactic skills. Bohman, Bedore, Peña, Mendez-Perez, and Gillam (2010) addressed the question of the role of language use in the proficiencies of young bilingual children, which controlled to a degree for maturational factors. They found that kindergarteners' usage of each of their languages was related to abilities in both languages. Specifically, increased usage of English was correlated with higher English semantic and morphosyntactic abilities, and greater usage of Spanish was related to higher Spanish abilities in those areas.

3.4.2 Language Use and L1 Attrition or Loss

Language use is a primary factor in the continuing maintenance of L1, as well as for L2 acquisition. It is generally accepted that when contact with, exposure to, and use of a language are lost or decreased, the attrition process commences

(Bylund, 2009). In discussing the impact of language use/exposure on attrition, Dominguez (2018) noted two types of attrition. The first is attrition resulting in decreased levels of activation of L1, with cross-linguistic competition. The second type is the attrition seen in the actual linguistic structures of L1, where, as Dominguez noted, structures may appear to be "restructur[ed]" (p. 686). These changes give an appearance of flawed competence, as mentioned by Herdina and Jessner (2013), although they clarified that this type of linguistic restructuring does not occur in all bilinguals, or at least it does not occur in a linear fashion over time. They elaborated a definition of attrition as "the reduction or simplification of language systems and/or the impairment of access to them, which is furthermore assumed to be a normal, and frequently inevitable, aspect of language development and change during the lifespan of a multilingual speaker" (p. 753).

In addressing the impact of use on attrition in L1 grammar, Montrul (1999) indicated that changes in the amount of input (time spent hearing/using the language) may have a greater impact on L1 than the timing of exposure to L2. In other words, decreased time in L1 may be more significant for L1 loss than the age at which L2 introduction occurs. When input in/use of what initially was the primary language is interrupted or significantly reduced, there may be resulting changes in aspects of language such as verb morphology, use of auxiliaries, and syntax. As previously noted, L1 accent is also impacted by the amount of language use. Yeni-Komshian et al. (2000) conducted a study demonstrating that balanced use of two languages was more likely to result in average proficiency in L1 and L2 pronunciation. The authors observed that young English language learners may not retain native-like L1 pronunciation, which they attributed to decreased frequency of use of L1. de Leeuw, Tusha, and Schmid (2018) demonstrated that it is possible for older L2 acquirers to also demonstrate attrition of segmental and prosodic elements of L1, supporting the argument that amount of use is a strong influencer in this area.

A likely confounding variable in discussions of the impact of language use (including exposure) on L1 is the factor of L2 contact. As already discussed, time spent hearing and using L2 reduces the time spent hearing and using L1; this partial replacement of L1 input with input from another language has been linked to L1 attrition in a number of studies as summarized by Dominguez (2013). Beyond "contact time," Dominguez noted that exposure to L2 exerts "linguistic pressure" on L1 (p. 166), which can result in cross-linguistic influences on L1. Dominguez describes the different phenomena associated with this process (borrowing of L2 elements in L1; convergence of L1 and L2 structures; L1 restructuring); lexical, grammatical, and syntactic elements of language are all vulnerable to this type of influence.

Because the occurrence of such "linguistic pressure" happens during periods of increased L2 use/decreased L1 use, it is difficult to separate the effects of decreased time in the language from the effects of L2 influence on L1. Some insight may be gained by reviewing the literature indicating that complete language loss has been observed only in cases of pre-pubertal attrition; it appears that the L1 of older attriters is not as influenced by the amount of time spent in the L2 setting (Dominguez, 2013). As with all other aspects of bilingual language proficiency, it must be noted that attrition is influenced by a number of other psychosocial and contextual variables, including level of education, individual differences, and affective factors; these further fog the role that language use plays in L1 attrition.

3.4.3 Language Use and Cognitive/Cortical Effects in Bilingual Speakers

Evidence from neuroscience shows the impact of language use on L1 and L2, perhaps more consistently than does the behavioral evidence from the field of linguistics. Speaking in a general sense, it is believed that cortical maps are created by L1 representations; repeated language use is deemed to solidify these mappings and cause them to be resistant to restructuring. However, theoretically these mappings can become deactivated by decreased use, allowing the underlying structures to be utilized in establishing L2 knowledge (Bylund, 2018). Thus, L1 restructuring is associated with neurocognitive processes that happen in the context of deactivation due to reduced use. de Bot (2018) observed that the system restructuring resultant from language non-use is unpredictable, and the changes non-linear; it appears that a similar observation can be made about changes due to decreased language use and exposure.

Reportedly, the deactivation process secondary to changes in language exposure may be observed in delays demonstrated in L1 response times, apparently due to cognitive pressures caused when L2 becomes dominant. Even late bilingual speakers may demonstrate such effects on L1 if the preponderance of language use shifts toward L2 (Dominguez, 2018; Köpke, 2003). Cognitive effects of attrition related to decreased use include poorer L1 lexical retrieval speeds (Schmid, Köpke, & de Bot, 2013). This effect in L1 has been noted even in non-fluent L2 speakers after a one-semester study abroad program where exposure to and use of L1 were significantly modified over a limited period of time (Baus, Costa, & Carreiras, 2013).

Consonni et al. (2013) included language exposure as an independent variable in their fMRI study comparing levels of L1/L2 neuroconvergence. The study compared groups of simultaneous bilinguals and early sequential bilinguals with AOAs of between three and six years ("late" bilinguals were not included) on language comprehension and noun/verb production tasks in Friulian and Italian. Both groups were highly proficient in the two languages. Friulian was considered the L1 of the sequential bilinguals and the "less exposed" language for all speakers; both groups were more exposed to Italian. In summarizing their findings, the authors noted that results pointed toward neural convergence for language comprehension for both groups. However, they found that for all subjects, the left thalamus was recruited in language comprehension of the less exposed language, Friulian.

> Thalamic engagement was evidenced also during Friulian LC [language comprehension] independently of group . . . the left thalamic activation was related to the less-exposed language (Friulian). These [*sic*] finding suggests that the left thalamus might support the processing of the less-exposed language even if it is L1 as it was for the HPLA group . . . It is possible that the left thalamus has a role in language selection process and control. (p. 1257)

In summary, neuroimaging evidence indicates that language exposure affects the pattern of brain activation in word production, even if speakers show comparable levels of proficiency in both (all) languages. Furthermore, decreased exposure to L1 reduces controlled processing capacity for that language, even in simultaneous bilingual speakers.

3.5 The Effects of L1 on L2 Acquisition and Proficiency

While relationships have long been established between L2 proficiency and the variables of AOA and frequency of L2 use, interest is growing in the topic of the influence of L1 proficiency on L2 acquisition. This relationship has been the focus of much scrutiny in the field of bilingual education: A large-scale program evaluation (Ramirez et al., 1991) examining outcomes for students enrolled in different types of language programming (none/ESL/bilingual education) found a consistent, positive relationship between the amount of L1 support and exposure, and outcomes in L2 English (specifically in reading comprehension and other academic language measures). In reflecting on these outcomes, proponents of bilingual education have suggested that higher levels of development in L1 have permitted students to be more successful in acquiring complex language skills in English.

In a later study, Flege et al. (1999) found that some late L2 learners demonstrated highly proficient grammatical skills in their L2. They attributed this finding to the notion that a more developed set of L1 representations will have a greater influence on how the representations of an L2 become established.

Similarly, Eubank and Gregg (1999) suggested that the late L2 learners in their study were successful in acquiring English grammatical skills because they were basing their responses on L1 knowledge combined with possibly advanced metalinguistic skills. It would appear from review of these earlier studies that a high degree of L1 proficiency provides a foundation for increased L2 proficiency; however, before arriving at this conclusion it is important to determine how proficiency is defined or operationalized in each study, as each may be looking at different aspects of language skill, including elements of accent, grammar, semantic/lexical ability, or cognitive/cortical control.

One issue which clouds the question of the degree to which L1 proficiency impacts L2 proficiency (in considering positive effects) is that of the confound of general language aptitude *in highly proficient bilinguals*. Simply considering the chronology of the acquisition process, one might assume that the first developed language would impact the second (acquired) language; however, the confound is that some speakers are highly proficient sequential bilinguals because they have the individual capacity to learn languages very well. Therefore, in bilinguals who are very proficient in both languages it is not safe to assume that a strong L1 laid the foundation for excellent L2 acquisition. For example, Delcenserie and Genesee (2017) found an advantage for bilinguals over monolinguals in tests of verbal and nonverbal WM: Might these skills noted in such a group reflect a general aptitude for learning language? DeKeyser et al. (2010) further point out that most of the research done in the area of proficiency has involved convenience samples of highly educated participants, which might be considered to reflect a population skewed toward above-average language abilities. With the confound being acknowledged, does L1 provide a foundation for L2 language acquisition in some aspects of acquisition?

3.5.1 L1 Effects on L2 Linguistic Behaviors

Studies in three areas (accent, grammar, and semantics) provide insight into the effects of L1 on acquired L2 proficiency as observed in assessments of skill. An inevitable conclusion is that L1 language behaviors have an impact on L2 language behaviors; the degree and direction of the impact are variable and appear to relate (depending on which element is under scrutiny) to already discussed variables AOA and language use (Bylund, 2018).

One frequently reviewed topic in this area is the tendency of bilingual speakers to transfer elements from one language to the other while speaking. Francis (2012) provided a thorough discussion of cross-linguistic transfer in his comprehensive text on bilingual language development. There he noted that in balanced bilinguals (individuals who demonstrate complete or age-appropriate development in all language systems in both languages), L1 to L2 transfers in the more finite and "complete" (p. 117) structural systems of phonology and morphosyntax tend to be temporary. In support of Francis' dual language system hypothesis, the structural components of the two languages are separate. More persistent structural borrowing occurs when and to the degree that there is an imbalance in language acquisition; persistent error patterns appear in the non-dominant, developmentally incomplete language. Errors typically consist of transfer of structural elements from the dominant language; in other words, frequent transfers *into* a language indicate lesser development or acquisition *of* that language.

As noted, Francis described the structural elements of language as not shared by the two languages because these systems are learned automatically and "encapsulated." On the other hand, Francis denoted the lexical/semantic system as based on domain-general abilities, and as a result is open and shared between the two languages. Therefore, lexical or conceptual development in either language makes knowledge available to the other (see Francis, 2012, for a comprehensive discussion).

The L2 phonological system appears to be particularly sensitive to L1 influence. Kartushina et al. (2016) provided a brief review of the subject. These authors summarized studies indicating that simultaneous and very early bilinguals are able to separate and accommodate the phonetic categories of both their languages, whereas late bilinguals (acquiring L2 after the age of 8) tend to merge similar cross-language sounds into one category. Phonemes in L2 are thus assimilated, in production, to similar L1 phonemes, the result being a phonology that is clearly distinct from that of a monolingual speaker of the language (or a simultaneous bilingual speaker) – in other words, an accent.

Similarly, Prior, Degani, Awawdy, Yassin, and Korem (2017) found L1 influences on L2 syntactic skills in highly proficient Arabic-Hebrew bilinguals when compared to Hebrew-speaking monolinguals. On a Hebrew grammaticality judgment task participants experienced more difficulty than controls in accurately processing Hebrew sentences with grammatical structures that were significantly different from Arabic. Outcomes for semantic/lexical tasks also showed decreased accuracy and slower reaction times for responses to false Hebrew cognates. The authors summarized: "we observed robust cross-language interference, [L1 to L2] in both lexicon and grammar, for proficient adult different-script bilinguals" (p. 22).

This sample from recent studies on the topic of L1 impact on L2 reflects a general trend of findings (based on behavioral results) of L1 to L2 interference, with implications being that L1 provides competition or interference rather than support for L2 proficiency. Another perspective about L1 impact on L2 performance will be discussed in Section 3.5.3.

3.5.2 L1 Impact on L2: Cognitive and Cortical Evidence

It has been established by behavioral and imaging studies that both languages of sequential bilingual speakers are active in the brain when the speaker is utilizing L2 (Marian, Spivey, & Hirsch, 2003). It has been posited in this regard that L1 serves as a mediator, or translator, for L2 comprehension and use (Thierry et al., 2007). On the other hand, coactivation of L2 (when speaking L1) is related to L2 proficiency – in other words, likely to occur during L1 use to the degree that the speaker is highly proficient in L2.

In looking at the brain structures involved, Consonni et al. (2013) found that in general the same neural resources/structures are utilized by early and late highly proficient bilinguals (matched for proficiency) on bilingual listening comprehension and noun and verb production. However, there is an effect for differences in language proficiency on L1 and L2 activation as seen in neuroimaging. Marian, Bartolotti, Rochanavibhata, Bradley, and Hernandez (2017) noted, in an fMRI study of bilingual patterns of brain activation during between- and within-language tasks, that "even within our group of highly proficient bilinguals, the activation of subcortical structures was found to be related to small differences in proficiency," with less dominant L2 recruiting additional structures over what was seen during L1 performance.

3.5.3 The BICS/CALP Model of Language Proficiency: L1 to L2 Effects?

It may be surprising that Francis (2012) described language transfer as a principal resource for the L2 learner for the task of acquiring an L2. In light of the discussion above, how can this be accurate? For which types of language abilities might this be true? Francis wrote within the framework of a modular theory of bilingual language skills (viewing the language skills of bilingual speakers as generally separate and distinct from one another, while acknowledging the occurrence of language transfer). He distinguished between "linguistic knowledge components" (p. 53), which are specific to each language, and "language-independent" (p. 52) knowledge, which he connected with Cummins' (1991) construct of CUP.

In order to comprehend the role that CUP may play in the puzzle of how L1 impacts L2 abilities, it is necessary to explore Cummins' (1981) earlier work. Cummins postulated that language proficiency is actually a dichotomy of skills, with a distinction being made between basic interpersonal communication skills (BICS) and cognitive/academic language proficiency (CALP).

BICS involves comprehending and using language within interpersonal, context-embedded situations. The features of BICS are those visible surface language proficiencies of pronunciation, basic vocabulary and grammar. CALP, on the other hand, though emerging from BICS, requires the ability to manipulate or reflect upon those features (metalinguistic knowledge) and the ability to use and understand language in decontextualized academic situations. As such, CALP is strongly related to literacy skills. However, BICS and CALP are related. CALP emerges from BICS. Language assessment which merely measures BICS can give a misleading impression of an individual's overall linguistic proficiency.

At this point in Cummins' (1981) model the role of "common underlying proficiency," or linguistic interdependence, can be understood. In the model, CALP ability is seen as shared between languages, and competence in the L2 (L2) becomes possible because the common underlying proficiency allows skill transfer from the L1 to L2. Transferred skills might include comprehension/development of abstract concepts, or metalinguistic skills such as the ability to analyze a grammatical form or phonetically sound out a word. Such transfer, occurring because of a hypothesized "linguistic interdependence," would mean that individuals with well-developed social and academic language skills in L1 should develop high levels of competence in L2, depending on their level of exposure to the new language.

An example of a study connecting proficiency outcomes to this model, in addition to those referenced earlier, is seen in Jiang and Kuehn (2001). In their examination of academic language outcomes, late immigrant students generally made better progress than early immigrant students in the comprehension and use of English. The authors posited that this finding was due to the transfer of earlier learned linguistic/metalinguistic knowledge and cognitive skills from L1 to L2.

In response, then, to the earlier posed question regarding the consideration of language transfer from L1 to L2 as a resource for L2 acquirers, Francis (2012) differentiated between "transfer" as used in the bilingual education literature when referring to the interaction between L1 and L2, and "transfer" as employed in the discipline of SLA. In the latter, the term "transfer" refers to the interaction between language subsystems. Cummins and other theorists interested in the educational implications of bilingualism used "transfer" to refer to shared resources (the previously mentioned interdependence) between the two languages, as developed in the CUP construct. In the sense that L1 develops prior to L2 for sequential bilinguals, L1 is the means through which much or most of this knowledge, a resource later available to L2, is originally acquired.

Francis (2012) refined the BICS/CALP/CUP model to specify the makeup of CUP, seeking to expand it while making a "more explicit separation between linguistic and conceptual domains" (p. 56). He referenced CUP as a central operating system (borrowing from Baker, 2006, as previously discussed), focusing on its role as a single "integrated source of thought" (p. 57). The key notion promoted in this discussion is that the "competencies that underlie discourse ability, text comprehension, and general language-processing skills are not language-bound" (p. 58).

Francis (2012) provided a critical analysis of the BICS/CALP model in his text, noting that critics have described the concept of CALP as a narrow view of proficiency, related entirely to classroom performance and therefore not available to speakers who lack access to education. Those providing this critique noted that the model lends itself to a deficit view of the language skills of those speakers who do not have the opportunity to develop academic language proficiency. Cummins (2008) returned in later years with rebuttals of this criticism and a refining of the model.

A modification of the model based on those early critiques was proposed by Francis (2012) in which he argued for a division of types of proficiency based on the timeline and automaticity with which kinds of language skill are learned. He termed these different proficiency types *primary* and *secondary discourse abilities*. He explained: "The distinction between conversational (primary) discourse ability and literacy-related, academic-type (secondary) discourse ability has been useful in understanding different kinds of variation in language use" (p. 104). Francis expanded the concept of CALP (or secondary discourse abilities) to include, for example, robust vocabulary developed through a community's oral tradition. In doing so he de-emphasized the "academic language" emphasis while acknowledging that the skills in question go beyond the attainment of a complete, basic grammar. He noted that there should be significant individual variation in these secondary discourse abilities (which do include written language abilities, higher-order comprehension skills, and metalinguistic awareness, as in the original CALP model). In Francis' clarification of the BICS/CALP continuum, secondary discourse skills are a late-developing type of language ability that are not developmentally "closed" but "open in relation to time and maturation" (p. 94). Francis acknowledged that the boundaries between primary and secondary discourse abilities are hypothetical; there are aspects of a complex grammar beyond a language's "core grammar" (p. 201) that may be learned at a secondary discourse level, perhaps because these involve general-learning mechanisms to permit comprehension and use.

In returning to the question of the impact of L1 on the development of primary discourse skills (BICS), and then secondary discourse skills (CALP) in L2 (for sequential bilinguals), it can be noted that while the abilities in the CUP (conceptual abilities) are not specifically related to the linguistic code spoken, chronologically they are learned through the vehicle of comprehensible input in L1 and then become accessible to the L2. Coming full circle, we return in this context to the question of the impact of age on L2 language proficiency. Krashen, Long, and Scarcella (1979), in their early development of the theory of cognitive and academic language skills, agreed that older language learners have an initial advantage over younger learners because of cross-linguistic transfer. However, they noted that in the long run young language learners tend to achieve higher levels of ultimate language attainment, other factors being equal. To date, this conclusion has not been disconfirmed.

4 What Are the New Avenues for Research?

A new avenue for work in this area explores the effects of L1 CALP. As such, a study designed in light of the variables discussed above was conducted among 82 adult Spanish-English bilinguals, all identifying Spanish as their L1 and English as their L2. The focus of the study was to evaluate the impact of L1 CALP (or secondary discourse skills) on the attainment of L2 proficiency (using as a point of departure the notion that skills developed in L1 should serve as a resource for some L2 abilities). The study also investigated how the primary variables of interest to the SLA field (AOA and use) factor into the degree of L2 attainment achieved. Finally, the impact of those factors was studied in L1, seeking to understand "how different language components interact within and across languages when accessed by a bilingual mind" (Sanchez, 2017, p. 754).

Specific independent variables that were considered were: AOA, amount of early exposure to L1 and L2, and current patterns of use in L1 and L2. CALP in L1 was utilized as both an independent and dependent variable. Dependent variables included: ratings of accent in L2, L1 and L2 grammatical abilities (production tasks), and L1 and L2 CALP as demonstrated in metalinguistic tasks (verbal analogies) and advanced vocabulary assessment. L1 and L2 grammar were viewed as both primary discourse skills (BICS) and possibly secondary discourse abilities (CALP). The aspect of grammar measured in L1 (Spanish) was the capacity of the individual to produce later developing, advanced verb forms (these forms were considered as an element of secondary discourse abilities due to their lower frequency of appearance in many Spanish dialects) (Centeno & Cairns, 2010; Gallego & Marks 2015). In English the grammatical skills of interest were the production of regular (primary discourse) and irregular (secondary discourse) past tense. Methods by which each variable was defined and measured will be discussed later in this section.

The following questions were identified to examine these relationships:

1. In L2 (English), to what extent do AOA, amount of use (early/late), and L1 CALP predict proficiency in accent?
2. In L2 (English), to what extent do AOA, amount of early exposure/late use, and L1 CALP predict English past tense production (regular and irregular past tense)?
3. To what extent do AOA and amount of early exposure/late use predict L1 CALP?
4. To what extent do AOA, amount of early exposure/late use, and L1 CALP predict L1 (Spanish) advanced verb production ability?
5. To what extent do AOA and amount of early exposure/late use predict Spanish CALP?

4.1 Research Design Challenges in Studying Bilingual Language Proficiency

Conceptual and methodological challenges have complicated research on the topics of bilingualism and L2 acquisition. First, definitions of language proficiency have varied widely and have been operationalized according to different language competencies (examples: grammatical comprehension or vocabulary scope). Often researchers wish to focus on the abilities of "native speakers," and yet, as Bialystok and Hakuta (1999) pointed out, there is no clear definition of the notion of "native-like" proficiency. The assumption is that such proficiency is an ideal; however, it is difficult to designate as a standard for linguistic performance, realizing that even native speakers may have varying proficiency levels according to the aspect of language being measured. Based on these concerns, Bialystok and Hakuta called for researchers to increase the "explanatory precision" (p. 166) of their theories, including specific structures or components of language that theoretically would be impacted by the variables in question.

A methodological issue with a number of studies is the tendency to use categorical measures to group language users into categories of "high proficiency/low proficiency." Viewing proficiency as a dichotic or categorical variable limits the power of statistical analysis to grade the effects that other factors may have on proficiency as an outcome. Likewise, such treatment of proficiency in studies may constrain understanding of the impact that gradations in proficiency have on other outcome variables.

4.2 CALP as a Continuous Variable

In contrast, aspects of CALP lend themselves to standardized assessment, providing scores of a sort that can be utilized as a continuous variable. An example of such a CALP measure is the Woodcock–Munoz Language Survey Normative Update (WMLS-NU; Woodcock & Munoz-Sandoval, 2001). Per the test manual, the measure assesses "aspects of language proficiency that emerge and become distinctive with formal schooling" (p. 3). The test is available in English and Spanish forms; each form comprised of two subtests: (1) Picture Vocabulary (including items selected from the academic curriculum such as "pyramid, sphinx, and printing press") and (2) Verbal Analogies skill (requiring use of metalinguistic, inductive reasoning). These provide a cluster score (standard score) that is on a continuous scale, allowing the user to see greater variance in a population for the skills assessed (as opposed to merely assigning the subjects to categories of proficiency based on their performance). The measure demonstrates strong reliability and validity indices (Woodcock & Munoz-Sandoval, 2001), with split-half reliability ranging from .80 to .93 for subtests and .88 to .96 for clusters. As this study incorporates the construct of CALP, the WMLS-NU provides a standardized, continuous CALP measure against which to compare results from researcher-constructed tools.

4.3 Purpose and Design of the Exploratory Study

This study, then, sought to explore the interdependent nature of the two languages of Spanish-English bilingual speakers, using as continuous variables the outcomes of well-developed measures of cognitive and academic language proficiency (Cummins, 1981; Woodcock & Muñoz-Sandoval, 2001). The Spanish and English editions of the WMLS, described more fully below, provide standardized "measuring sticks" against which to compare researcher-constructed measures of English (L2) and Spanish (L1) grammar and English accent. In this manner, the interactions of the variables of AOA of L2, frequency of use of each language, and degrees of proficiency in each language were assessed within the context of the bilingual speakers' language systems.

4.3.1 Participants

Participants were 82 Spanish-English bilingual students (ages 18–48 years) recruited from general psychology, educational psychology, and human development and family studies classes held on the campus of a large urban university. The criterion for inclusion as a participant in the study was having Spanish, learned prior to the age of 3, as the L1 spoken. (Participants all self-identified as L1 speakers of Spanish.) English was the L2 each subject learned to speak. The sample consisted of 66 females (80%) and 16 males (20%). The mean age of the participants was 23.11 years (*SD* = 5.58). Within the group of participants, 44 (53%) were born in the United States, while 38 (47%) immigrated to the United States from another country. Participants who completed all phases of the data collection process for this study were awarded extra-credit certificates that could be utilized in their academic classes.

4.3.2 Instruments Used for Predictor Variables

A revised version of the Language Background Questionnaire (Flege & McKay, 2004) was completed by each participant (see Appendix A). This questionnaire is a self-report of personal data that asks the respondent to provide information about the age at which English (L2) was acquired. In the latter section of the questionnaire, the respondents estimate the percentage of time spent speaking Spanish and English in a variety of activities and settings. This questionnaire and others similar to it have been utilized in a variety of studies assessing impact of AOA and language use (Flege & McKay, 2004; Guion, Flege, & Loftin, 2000; Silverberg & Samuel, 2004; Wartenberger et al., 2003). For the version of the questionnaire utilized in this study, two additional questions reflecting the number of years of education in each language were added. Furthermore, the original questionnaire addressed only L1 in the section requiring estimates of percentage of language use. For this study an identical section addressing L2 (English) was added. Demographic information, including gender, age, and country of origin, was also collected on the questionnaire.

4.3.2.1 Age of Acquisition

In order to assess the impact that AOA and frequency of language usage had on bilingual language skills, data representing these variables were extracted from the questionnaire. One of these, AOA of L2, was defined as the age of arrival to the L2 environment. Therefore, while all of the participants reported speaking Spanish as an L1 and learning to speak English after the age of 3 (sequential bilingual speakers), those who were born in the United States were recorded as having an arrival age of 0. This reflected their early environmental exposure to the English language, a factor determined by previous studies (Johnson & Newport, 1989) to be relevant to outcomes of interest in this study, such as accent. A bivariate correlation was calculated between age of arrival and the AOA of English reported by the participants, $r(82) = .64, p < .001$, indicating a moderately strong, positive, statistically significant relation between the two measures of AOA.

4.3.2.2 Language Exposure (early) and Use (Recent/Current)

In order to examine the impact of language use it was deemed important to address degree of early exposure and recent usage (past five years) of the two languages. Early language exposure was represented by the number of years of education speakers had in each language (i.e., educational programming that was delivered in the target language). This was judged to be a reasonable indicator of amount of language exposure during developmental years, as children receiving education delivered in the Spanish language would hear the language more hours per day than those receiving education delivered in English and vice versa. For some participants, years of education in Spanish occurred in another country (and was provided in a monolingual context), and for some, education in Spanish occurred in the United States during participation in a bilingual educational program. In the study, participants were simply asked to note the number of years in which educational programming was provided to them in each language.

In order to determine the extent to which each language was used during the past five years, participants were asked to provide estimated percentages of time (0–100%) that they spoke Spanish, then later English, in each of a range of settings. These included: home, work, class, phone conversations, visits to friends and family members, church, vacation, shopping trips, and parties/social gatherings. Although in the instructions the participants were advised to consider the two languages together when estimating, it was noted that many had difficulty reporting percentages and therefore over- or under-estimated total speaking time. In other words, total speaking time for a setting as reported by a participant may have added up to more or less than 100%. To account, then, for use of each language, the following procedure was utilized: (1) For each language the percentages per category were added together and an average was taken; (2) the two averages were summed and the total was accepted as representing total speaking time; and (3) the proportions of the total represented by the original averages for each language were calculated. This resulted in two measures, an estimated proportion of English use for the past five years and a corresponding proportion of Spanish use for the past five years.

4.3.2.3 Cognitive and Academic Language Proficiency

The WMLS-NU (English and Spanish forms) (Woodcock & Munoz-Sandoval, 2001) was utilized to assess general levels of cognitive and academic proficiency in each language. This standardized measure of Spanish and English proficiency provides parallel test forms in the two languages. The test manual provides strong reliability and validity indices supporting the use of this measure to assess CALP in Spanish and English, as previously described, with median split-half reliability coefficients ranging from .88 to .96. The raw scores (number of correct responses) for the picture vocabulary and verbal analogies subtests in English and Spanish were entered into the computer-scoring program. The program generated standard scores representing the English and Spanish oral language proficiency, or CALP, of each participant. Spanish CALP served as a predictor for the language skills of interest, and was also assessed as an outcome of the variables of age of arrival and early and recent language use. English CALP was utilized as a predictor in a number of post hoc analyses.

4.3.2.4 Perceptual/Thinking Skills

Finally, effects of variability in the cognitive skills of the examinees were controlled by administration of the *Standard Progressive Matrices (SPM), 1998 edition* (Raven, Raven, & Court, 1998), a nonverbal assessment of perception and thinking skills. The test manual yields information from over 40 studies regarding the reliability of the measure across age ranges and cultural groups. In general, these studies provide documentation indicating solid indices of internal consistency and retest reliability. Regarding validity indices, results on the SPM have been positively correlated with the *Wechsler Adult Intelligence Scale-Revised* in a number of studies (Raven et al. 1998). The measure requires that examinees complete figures and patterns containing blank spaces by selecting another pattern piece from a range of choices that best fits the empty area. Scores on this measure were standard percentile ranks.

4.3.3 Instruments Used for Language Outcome Measures

4.3.3.1 English Accent

English accent was assessed by asking participants to read aloud a standard, four-sentence paragraph that contains most of the consonants, vowels, and consonant clusters of the English language. The elicitation paragraph, labeled Accent Rating Paragraph (see Appendix B), was taken from the Speech Accent Archive website, a product of the linguistics department of George Mason University. The reading samples were recorded for accent rating using a digital tape recorder. Two trained adult raters who were native speakers of English rated each performance using a five-point scale, with the endpoints of the scale being "no accent" (number 1) and "very strong accent" (number 5). Although previous studies of accent (Yeni-Komshian et al., 2000) have utilized a nine-point scale for rating extent of accent, it was determined that a five-point scale provided an adequate range of ordinal ranks for differentiating accents while being more accessible to raters (Friedman & Amoo, 1999). Once the samples were rated, rating values were transposed so that lower values indicated less "native-like" accent and higher values indicated a more "native-like" accent.

Raters were trained by listening to non-test samples of bilingual Spanish-English speakers reading the test paragraph. The five points of the rating scale were discussed and example recordings were utilized to illustrate the full range of ratings. Examples included readings from monolingual English speakers and bilingual speakers of English with varying degrees proficiency. Raters were directed to take the full scale into account when considering the rating for any one example. Raters were then asked to rate groups of ten sample readings and consensus/reliability indices were calculated. Training concluded when, following three rounds of sample rating, a high degree of consensus was demonstrated with a Spearman Rho correlation of .85. For the study ratings, inter-rater consensus was .80, and internal consistency was indicated by an alpha of .89. The score for this outcome measure was the average of the ratings obtained for each speaker.

4.3.3.2 English Regular and Irregular Past Tense Production

Production of English past tense forms was assessed with the English Past Tense Test (researcher-constructed; see Appendix C) in which examinees heard a set of English verbs and then responded with the indicated past tense forms. The past tense grammar target was chosen based on data that indicate that English past tense formation is prone to dialectical variation in speakers with limited English proficiency (Goldstein, 2000). The verb list, consisting of 80 verbs, was controlled for word frequency, verb regularity, and type of past tense formation (Bird et al., 2003; Ullman, 1999). The measure consisted of 20 high-frequency verbs requiring an irregular past tense form, and 60 high-frequency verbs taking regular past tense forms. Regular past tense ending (which in written language takes the form of "ed") is produced verbally as a final /t/, final /d/, or final /ɪd/. Twenty words from each of these categories were selected for the regular past tense portion of the measure.

The past tense measure yielded two scores: one score for regular past tense production (total out of 60) and one for irregular past tense production (total out of 20). Scores from the two subtests (irregular verbs and regular verbs) were utilized as outcomes instead of a total test score. Internal reliability for this measure was calculated by obtaining Cronbach's alphas for the two subtests (irregular verbs and regular verbs); they were .84 and .91, respectively. Alpha for the entire measure was .92.

4.4.3.3 Spanish Verb Production

The Spanish Verb Test (researcher-constructed; see Appendix D) was utilized to assess examinees' skills in producing two later developing Spanish verb forms (Goldstein, 2000): the imperfect subjunctive and the conditional moods. These particular grammar targets were selected based on the implications of Anderson's (1999) case study, which indicated that later developing verb forms were more likely to be impacted by language attrition in bilingual speakers. The measure was composed of 40 items. Half of the items measured the target verb forms, and half measured the earlier developing forms (the present indicative and preterit past tense).

Each item consisted of an infinitive and an incomplete sentence. Subjects were required to complete the sentence with a form of the infinitive verb. Items were designed to elicit target verb forms and earlier developing verb forms (present and preterit past tense) in first and third person. Half of the sentences utilized verbs that take regular forms, and half included verbs that take irregular forms. To control for possible unfamiliarity with certain verbs, only high-frequency verbs were utilized in the measure. High-frequency verb classification was determined by selecting verbs from the site: *Los Cien Verbos Mas Usados en el Espanol* (The 100 Most Frequently Used Verbs in Spanish) (Brenchley & Brenchley, 2006). According to the site authors (bilingual translators and editors), Spanish verb frequency was evaluated by conducting a computerized frequency count of verbs in a large sample of Spanish text, including novels and other source material (J. Brenchley, personal communication, October 9, 2006).

This measure was developed by the researcher in consultation with adults who are native speakers of Spanish. Once developed, items were checked for grammaticality by a professor of Spanish at a liberal arts university. The test was then piloted in two stages to determine if the sentences consistently elicited the target structures. Stage-one piloting involved administering the instrument to ten adult native speakers of Spanish. Responses indicated the need to rewrite seven of the 40 items in order to consistently prompt the desired responses (for these items the correct response rate was less than 70%). Adjustments were made and the measure was piloted again with ten adults who are native speakers of Spanish. Responses on the second stage of testing indicated that in its new form the measure was effective at eliciting the target verbs 80% of the time or more when the incomplete sentence items were presented with the infinitive first. The maximum possible score for advanced verb form production was 20. Internal reliability for the measure per Cronbach's alpha was .82; for the advanced verb subtest alone the alpha was .81.

4.3.3.4 Cognitive and Academic Language Proficiency

Standard scores on the English and Spanish versions of the WMLS-NU were utilized as representing CALP in each language. This measure, with a description of reliability indices, is described in the previous section. Models were developed predicting CALP in each language as an outcome. In the model predicting English CALP, Spanish CALP was included as a predictor variable.

4.4 Procedures

Participants were tested individually by trained examiners during two hour sessions. Detailed procedure guidelines were followed for each administration. Administration of the Bilingual Language Questionnaire, the Standard Progressive Matrices, and the WMLS-NU (Spanish and English versions) was completed at a table in a quiet testing room. Order of administration of the Spanish and English versions of the WMLS-NU was alternated for each examinee. Recording of the reading sample for accent rating also occurred in the testing room.

The Spanish advanced verb test and English past tense test were presented to the subjects orally via computer. Test items were recorded digitally; a native speaker of Spanish recorded Spanish-language items, and a native speaker of English-recorded English-language items. Items were randomly presented for each test during sessions.

Administration occurred in a sound-isolation testing booth, and stimuli were presented at a quiet conversational level. As the computer presented the test items, the examiner scored subject responses for accuracy. There was a three-second interval between items to allow for participant response. Order of presentation of the tests alternated with each examinee for purposes of counter-balancing any examiner error caused by repetitive testing order.

Hierarchical (sequential) regression analyses were utilized to examine the relations between the independent and dependent variables (see Plonsky & Ghandar, 2018, for discussion of the utility of hierarchical models in L2 acquisition research). Models were built in a roughly chronological framework beginning with the onset of L2 (English) acquisition. Subsequent variables were then entered as they would have occurred during the rest of the bilingual language acquisition process. In Step 1 of each regression, age of arrival was entered alone. In Step 2, this was followed by early language exposure, which in this study, was equivalent to years of education in English for English language outcomes, or years of education in Spanish for Spanish language outcomes. Proportion of English or Spanish language use, accordingly, in the past five years was entered in Step 3. In Step 4, Spanish CALP (L1 proficiency) was entered as an indicator of current level of language ability.

4.5 Results

Of the 82 participants, 6 individuals did not complete some portion of the full assessment; their data were included when possible for the variables addressed in specific models. The result was that means and standard deviations for predictors and outcomes varied slightly among regression models as all available data were included for each. Table 1 provides the means and standard deviations for all variables per model. Table 2 presents bivariate correlations for all variables as calculated for each regression model.

It should be noted that the original research design called for use of scores from the standard progressive matrices (SPM) as a control variable for perceptual/thinking skills. Bivariate correlations of SPM percentile ranks and the predictor and outcome variables indicated a low, statistically significant correlation, $r(79) = .29$, $p < .05$, with only one outcome variable, English CALP (cognitive and academic language proficiency). Because SPM scores did not correlate with any other predictors or outcomes, it was omitted from most of the hierarchical regressions in the interest of parsimony. It was, however, included in the one model addressing the outcome of English CALP.

An alpha of .05 was adopted due to the exploratory nature of the research, to lessen the risk of a Type 2 error. In each model of the study, the possibility of multicollinearity was addressed by examining tolerance and variance inflation factors. These were found in each case to be at acceptable levels, indicating that multicollinearity was not an issue.

4.5.1 Research Question 1: Accent in L2

As shown in Table 3, in Step 1 of the hierarchical regression model predicting L2 accent, age of arrival predicted 29% of the variance ($R^2 = .30$, adjusted $R^2 = .29$). The model was significant, $F(1, 77) = 32.59$, $p < .001$. Addition of early English exposure (years of English education) to the model in Step 2 resulted in a significant model, $F(2, 76) = 20.06$, $p < .001$. The 4.8% increment in R^2 was also significant, $F(1, 76) = 5.59$, $p < .05$, with the model now accounting for 33% of the variance ($R^2 = .35$, adjusted $R^2 = .33$). In Step 3, addition of proportion of English use (past five years) was added, and explained an additional 4.7% of the variance, $F(1, 75) = 5.76$, $p < .05$. The model remained significant, $F(3, 75) = 16.13$, and accounted for 37% of the variance ($R^2 = .39$, adjusted $R^2 = .37$). With the addition of Spanish CALP in Step 4, no additional variance was identified. The model was still significant, $F(3,75) = 12.11$, $p < .001$. The final model predicted a moderate 36% of the variance according to the adjusted R^2 (Plonsky & Ghanbar, 2018), which represents a large effect size (Cohen, 1988).

Table 1 Means and standard deviations of predictor and outcome variables per model.

L2 Accent (N = 79)	*Mean*	*SD*
Age of Arrival	4.77	6.53
Early English Exposure (years of education in English)	11.65	4.20
Proportion English Use (past 5 years)	.57	.16
Spanish CALP	86.41	7.89
English CALP	91.66	8.04
Accent Rating	3.39	1.01
English Regular and Irregular Past Tense (N = 77)		
Age of Arrival	4.71	6.51
Early English Exposure (years of education in English)	11.68	4.16
Proportion English Use (past 5 years)	.58	.16
Spanish CALP	86.22	7.90
English CALP	91.64	7.99
English Regular Past Tense	51.81	7.83
English Irregular Past Tense	15.49	4.12
Advanced Spanish Verbs (N = 76)		
Age of Arrival	4.77	6.53
Early Spanish Exposure (years of education in Spanish)	4.62	4.39
Proportion Spanish Use (past 5 years)	.42	.16
Spanish CALP	86.29	7.93
Advanced Spanish Verbs	14.30	3.67
English CALP (N = 79)		
Age of Arrival	4.77	6.53
Early English Exposure (years of education in English)	11.65	4.20
Proportion English Use (past 5 years)	.57	.16
Spanish CALP	86.41	7.89
Standard Progressive Matrices	41.82	25.73
English CALP	91.66	8.04
Spanish CALP (N = 78)		
Age of Arrival	4.83	6.55
Early Spanish Exposure (years of education in Spanish)	4.63	4.38
Proportion Spanish Use (past 5 years)	.43	.16
Spanish CALP	86.47	7.92

Table 2 Zero-order correlations for all variables per model.

L2 Accent	1	2	3	4	5	6	7
1. Age of Arrival	-	-.47**	-.27**	.55**	-.01	-.54**	-
2. Early English Exposure		-	.29**	-.28**	.24*	.45**	-
3. Proportion English Use			-	-.24*	.24*	.39**	-
4. Spanish CALP				-	.34**	-.28**	-
5. English CALP					-	.25*	-
6. Accent Rating						-	-

English Regular/Irregular Past Tense	1	2	3	4	5	6	7
1. Age of Arrival	-	-.45**	-.26*	.55**	.02	-.37**	-.16
2. Early English Exposure		-	.29**	-.27**	.27**	.41**	.32**
3. Proportion English Use			-	-.23*	.25**	.30**	.11
4. Spanish CALP				-	.34**	-.15	.12
5. English CALP					-	.41**	.44**
6. English Regular Past Tense						-	.55**
7. English Irregular Past Tense							-

Advanced Spanish Verbs	1	2	3	4	5	6	7
1. Age of Arrival	-	.65**	.27*	.56**	.35**	-	-
2. Early Spanish Exposure		-	.47**	.41**	.31**	-	-
3. Proportion Spanish Use			-	.23*	.20*	-	-
4. Spanish CALP				-	.47**	-	-
5. Advanced Spanish Verbs					-	-	-

Table 2 (cont.)

English CALP

	1	2	3	4	5	6	7
1. Age of Arrival	-	-.47**	-.27**	.55**	-.13	-.01	-
2. Early English Exposure	-	-	.29**	-.28**	-.01	.30**	-
3. Proportion English Use	-	-	-	-.24*	.23*	.24*	-
4. Spanish CALP	-	-	-	-	.06	.34**	-
5. Standard Progressive Matrices	-	-	-	-	-	.31**	-
6. English CALP	-	-	-	-	-	-	-

Spanish CALP

	1	2	3	4	5	6	7
1. Age of Arrival	-	.66**	.27**	.55**	-	-	-
2. Early Spanish Exposure	-	-	.46**	.41**	-	-	-
3. Proportion Spanish Use	-	-	-	.25*	-	-	-
4. Spanish CALP	-	-	-	-	-	-	-

Note. $*p < .05$; $**p < .01$.

Table 3 Hierarchical regressions predicting L2 accent.

Step 1			
Age of Arrival	−.08	.02	-.55***
Step 2			
Age of Arrival	−.07	.02	−.43***
Early English Use	.06	.03	.25*
Step 3			
Age of Arrival	−.06	.02	−.39***
Early English Use	.05	.03	.20
Proportion English Use	1.48	.62	.23*
Step 4			
Age of Arrival	−.07	.02	−.43**
Early English Use	.05	.03	.20
Proportion English Use	1.53	.63	.24*
Spanish CALP	.01	.02	.07
Post Hoc Step 4			
Age of Arrival	−.07	.02	−.42***
Early English Use	.04	.03	.15
Pro. English Use	1.28	.62	.20*
English CALP	.01	.01	.15

Notes. Adjusted $R^2 = .29, p < .001$ for Step 1; $R^2 \Delta = .05$, Adjusted $R^2 = .33, p < .001$ for Step 2; $R^2 \Delta = .05$, Adjusted $R^2 = .37, p < .001$ for Step 3; $R^2 \Delta = .00$, Adjusted $R^2 = .36$, $p < .001$ for Step 4; $R^2 \Delta = .02$, Adjusted $R^2 = .38, p < .001$ for Post Hoc Step 4.

Within the final model, age of arrival had the greatest weight ($\beta = -.43, p < .01$), negatively predicting accent. Proportion of English use followed ($\beta = .24, p < .05$). The weight for early English exposure ($\beta = .20$) approached significance with $p = .059$, The outcome indicates that individuals with younger "ages of arrival" to the United States (these include those who were born here, with an age of arrival of 0) who demonstrate higher proportions of English use are likely to demonstrate a more "native-like" accent in their L2, English. Amount of early English use may also play a role in attaining "native-like" accent. L1 cognitive and academic language skills did not contribute to English accent in this study.

In a post hoc analysis the issue of the impact of English CALP on English accent was addressed by adding English CALP, instead of Spanish CALP into the model at Step 4. This model was also significant, $F(4, 74) = 12.98, p < .001$; however, the addition of English CALP did not result in significant change in R^2 ($R^2 \Delta = .02$, $p = .12$). This model predicted 38 % of the variance in English accent according to the adjusted R^2. In comparing the post hoc model to the previous model, predicting 36% of the variance for accent, it is observed that English CALP adds little to the overall predictive power of the model (and adds no unique variance).

4.5.2 Research Question 2: English Regular and Irregular Past Tense

Models predicting outcomes for English past tense were then examined (see Table 4). Production of English regular past tense verbs was analyzed first, and again the chronological model for entering predictor variables was followed. In Step 1, age of arrival was entered and was significant, $F(1, 75) = 11.91$, $p = .001$. Age of arrival predicted 13% of the variance on regular past tense verbs ($R^2 = .14$, adjusted $R^2 = .13$). The variable ($\beta = -.37$, $p = .001$) demonstrated a negative relationship with regular past tense verb production, indicating that earlier arrivers tend to perform better on this task. Early English use was entered into the model at Step 2. The model remained significant, $F(2, 74) = 9.90$, $p < .001$), and predicted 19% of the variance. The 7% change in R^2 was significant, $F(1, 74) = 6.95$, $p < .05$, with early English use ($\beta = .31$, $p = .01$) and age of arrival ($\beta = -.23$, $p < .05$) both contributing unique variance to the model. In Step 3, proportion of English use (past five years) was entered but did not result in a significant change in R^2. Finally, Spanish CALP was entered at Step 4. It was not significant in the model, which now predicted a small portion, 20%, of the variance for English regular past tense, a medium effect size (Cohen, 1988). The model itself was significant, $F(4, 72) = 5.85$, $p < .001$). Examination of the unique contributions of each variable indicated that at this step, the impact of age of arrival only approached significance ($\beta = -.26$, $p = .054$) while early English use bore more responsibility for the variance ($\beta = .27$, $p < .05$). Spanish CALP apparently did not impact production of English regular past tense.

In the post hoc analysis, the impact of English CALP in production of English regular past tense verbs was examined by substituting it for Spanish CALP in Step 4 of the model above. This resulted in a significant increase in the predictive power of the model, with an R^2 increment of 10%, $F(1, 72) = 10.98$, $p < .001$. The model itself predicted a moderate 30% of the variance for English regular past tense ($R^2 = .34$, adjusted $R^2 = .30$), a medium effect size (Cohen, 1988), and was significant, $F(4, 72) = 9.21$, $p < .001$. The presence of English CALP affected the impact of early English exposure in the model, resulting in its no longer being significant ($\beta = .16$, $p = .15$). In this model, age of arrival ($\beta = -.28$, $p = < .05$) and English CALP ($\beta = .34$, $p = .001$) both contributed uniquely to the variance, indicating that early age of arrival positively impacts English regular verb production, while higher English CALP results in even better performance. This model is stronger than the previous model that did not take English CALP into account.

Competency in production of English irregular past tense verb forms was then examined, utilizing the same chronological model and variables. Step 1,

Table 4 Hierarchical regressions predicting English regular/irregular past tense production.

	English Regular Past Tense[a]			English Irregular Past Tense[b]		
	B	**SE B**	**β**	**B**	**SE B**	**β**
Step 1						
Age of Arrival	−.46	.13	−.37**	−.11	.07	−.17
Step 2						
Age of Arrival	−.28	.14	−.23*	−.02	.08	−.03
Early English Use	.58	.22	.31*	.30	.12	.31*
Step 3						
Age of Arrival	−.25	.14	−.20	−.02	.08	−.03
Early English Use	.51	.22	.27*	.30	.13	.30*
Pro. English Use	8.68	5.46	.17	.26	3.12	.01
Step 4						
Age of Arrival	−.31	.16	−.26	−.12	.09	−.19
Early English Use	.51	.22	.27*	.30	.12	.31*
Pro. English Use	9.14	5.50	.18	.97	3.03	.04
Spanish CALP	.11	.12	.11	.16	.07	.31*
Post Hoc Step 4 (REG)						
Age of Arrival	−.33	.13	−.28*	-	-	-
Early English Use	.31	.22	.16	-	-	-
Pro. English Use	4.89	5.25	.10	-	-	-
English CALP	.34	.10	.34**	-	-	-
Post Hoc Step 5 (IRR)						
Age of Arrival	-	-	-	−.10	.08	−.17
Early English Use	-	-	-	.19	.12	.20
Pro. English Use	-	-	-	−1.55	3.02	−.06
Spanish CALP	-	-	-	.06	.07	.12
English CALP	-	-	-	.19	.07	.36**

Notes. [a] Adjusted $R^2 = .13$, $p < .01$ for Step 1; $R^2 \Delta = .07$, Adjusted $R^2 = .19$, $p < .001$ for Step 2; $R^2 \Delta = .03$, Adjusted $R^2 = .20$, $p < .001$ for Step 3; $R^2 \Delta = .00$, Adjusted $R^2 = .20$, $p < .001$ for Step 4; $R^2 \Delta = .10$, Adjusted $R^2 = .30$, $p < .001$ for Post Hoc Step 4. **$p < .01$; *$p < .05$; $N = 77$.
[b] Adjusted $R^2 = .02$, $p = .15$ for Step 1; $R^2 \Delta = .07$, Adjusted $R^2 = .08$, $p < .05$ for Step 2; $R^2 \Delta = .00$, Adjusted $R^2 = .07$, $p < .05$ for Step 3; $R^2 \Delta = .07$, Adjusted $R^2 = .12$, $p < .01$ for Step 4; $R^2 \Delta = .09$, Adjusted $R^2 = .20$, $p < .01$ for Post Hoc Step 5. **$p < .01$; *$p < .05$; $N = 77$.

regression on age of arrival, did not yield a significant model. Addition of early English exposure at Step 2 did result in a significant model, $F(2, 74) = 4.18$, $p <.05$. This model predicted 8% of the variance ($R^2 = .10$, adjusted $R^2 = .08$). After entering proportion of English use at Step 3, the model was significant $F(3,73) = 2.75, p < .05$, but the change in R^2 was not significant. Finally, at step 4 Spanish CALP was added and resulted in a significant model, $F(4, 72) = 3.68$, $p <. 01$. The 6.8% change in R^2 was significant, $p < .05$. The model demonstrated a small effect size (12%) (Cohen, 1988), with $R^2 = .17$ and adjusted $R^2 = .12$. In this model, early English use and Spanish CALP contributed similarly to the variance. Their Beta weights were $\beta = .31$, $p < .05$ and $\beta = .31, p < .05$ respectively. Although predicting only a small portion of the variance (Plonsky & Ghanbar, 2018), this model indicated that higher levels of L1 CALP can result in higher performance in production of L2 irregular verbs. Results suggested that age of arrival has no effect on the accuracy of production of English irregular past tense.

Again, post hoc analysis was performed to investigate the impact of English CALP. Since Spanish CALP was significant in the previous model it remained as a predictor, and English CALP was entered at step 5. This final model predicted 20% of the variance, a medium effect size (Cohen, 1988), and was significant, $F(5, 71) = 4.86, p = .001$. In this model, English CALP was the only variable to demonstrate a significant weight ($\beta = .36, p < .01$). Spanish CALP was no longer significant at this step ($\beta = .12, p = .386$). Similarly, early English use was not significant when English CALP was taken into account ($\beta = .195$, $p = .118$). The results indicated that greater English CALP results in a higher degree of competency in the production of English irregular past tense forms, which was observed with regular past tense forms as well. Age of arrival did not appear to predict irregular forms though it did regular forms.

4.5.3 Research Question 3: Advanced Spanish Verb Production

In this model predicting skill in producing advanced Spanish verb forms, early Spanish exposure (as represented by years of education in Spanish) and proportion of Spanish use within the past five years were entered as predictors, as shown in Table 5. Age of arrival was the first variable entered at Step 1, and the resulting model was significant, $F(1, 74) = 10.44, p < .01$. Age of arrival predicted 11% of the variance for production of advanced verbs, a small effect size (Cohen, 1988), with $R^2 = .12$ and adjusted $R^2 = .11$. The positive relationship indicated that later arrivals demonstrated greater competence.

At Step 2, early Spanish exposure was added to the model, but the R^2 change of 2% was not significant, $F(1, 73) = 1.02, p = .32$. The model continued to be

Table 5 Hierarchical regressions predicting Spanish advanced verb production and Spanish CALP.

	Spanish Advanced Verbs[a]			Spanish CALP[b]		
	B	**SE B**	**β**	**B**	**SE B**	**β**
Step 1						
Age of Arrival	.20	.06	.35**	.66	.17	.55***
Step 2						
Age of Arrival	.14	.08	.26	.59	.16	.49***
Early Spanish Exposure	.12	.12	.15	.15	.25	.08
Step 3						
Age of Arrival	.15	.08	.26	.60	.16	.50***
Early Spanish Exposure	.08	.13	.10	.06	.25	.03
Proportion Spanish Use	2.02	2.91	.09	5.03	5.55	.10
Step 4						
Age of Arrival	.04	.08	.07	-	-	-
Early Span. Exp.	.07	.12	.08	-	-	-
Proportion Spanish Use	1.33	2.76	.06	-	-	-
Spanish CALP	.18	.06	.39**	-	-	-

Notes. [a] Adjusted $R^2 = .11$, $p < .01$ for Step 1; $R^2 \Delta = .01$, Adjusted $R^2 = .11$, $p < .01$ for Step 2; $R^2 \Delta = .01$, Adjusted $R^2 = .11$, $p < .05$ for Step 3; $R^2 \Delta = .11$, Adjusted $R^2 = .21$, $p < .001$ for Step 4; $N = 76$.
[b] Adjusted $R^2 = .29$, $p < .001$ for Step 1; $R^2 \Delta = .00$, Adjusted $R^2 = .28$, $p < .001$ for Step 2; $R^2 \Delta = .01$, Adjusted $R^2 = .28$, $p < .001$ for Step 3; $N = 78$.
*$p < .05$; **$p < .01$; ***$p < .001$.

significant, $F(2, 73) = 5.73$, $p < .01$. Similarly, in Step 3, addition of proportion of Spanish use in the past five years did not add to the model, with predictive power remaining at 11%. Also, no significant R^2 change occurred with the addition of that variable. In Step 4 of the model, Spanish CALP was added, and resulted in a significant R^2 change of 11%, $F(1, 71) = 9.99$, $p < .01$. The model then predicted a small portion, 21%, of total variance (a medium effect size) (Cohen, 1988), and was significant, $F(4, 71) = 5.83$, $p < .001$. In the final model, age of arrival was no longer significant as a predictor ($\beta = .07$, $p = .64$), and Spanish CALP was the only variable with significant weight in the model ($\beta = .39$, $p < .01$). The results suggested that individuals with higher levels of Spanish CALP are more likely to correctly produce advanced verb forms.

A post hoc analysis was conducted in an attempt to explain how individuals arrive at high levels of competency in production of advanced Spanish verbs.

A series of one-way ANOVAS was utilized to examine differences in group means. Subjects were grouped based on age of arrival (early ages 0–8 versus late ages 9 and above), amount of early exposure/years of Spanish education (0–5 years versus 6 or more years), and proportion of Spanish use in the past five years (0–.49 versus .5 and above). In the first analysis, group 2 (later arrivals, $N = 20$) demonstrated significantly greater competence in advanced verb production than did group 1 (early arrivals, $N = 60$), $F(1, 79) = 9.39$, $p < .01$. The mean score for group 1 was 13.42 (SD 4.08); for group 2 the mean was 16.4 (SD 2.58).

In the second analysis, group 2 (those with 6 or more years of Spanish education, $N = 25$) outperformed group 1 (those with 0–5 years of Spanish education, $N = 54$), $F(1, 79) = 4.82$, $p < .05$. Mean scores for group 1 and group 2 were 13.46 (SD 4.05) and 15.52 (3.47) respectively. In the final analysis of the series, group differences in proportion of Spanish use within the past five years did not result in significantly different scores on the advanced verb measure. Means for group 1 ($N = 50$) and group 2 ($N = 29$) were 13.84 (SD 3.96) and 15.21 (SD 2.896). All three analyses met the standard for Levene's test of homogeneity of group variances.

4.5.4 Research Question 4: English CALP

In the model predicting English CALP (see Table 6), age of arrival was entered at Step 1. The model was not significant, $F(1, 77) = .012$, $p = .91$. At Step 2, early English exposure was entered, and resulted in a significant model, $F(2, 76) = 4.67$, $p < .05$. The model predicted 9% of the variance, with $R^2 = .109$ and adjusted $R^2 = .86$. At step 3, proportion of English use was entered; the model was still significant, $F(3. 75) = 4.25$, $p < .01$, but the 3.6% change in R^2 was not significant. Spanish CALP was entered at Step 4, and resulted in a significant model, $F(4, 74) = 9.72$, $p < .001$, predicting 31% of the variance of English CALP (with $R^2 = .34$ and adjusted $R^2 = .309$). The R^2 change of 20% was significant, $F(1,74) = 22.48$, $p < .001$. At this step, three variables contributed uniquely to the variance. These were early English exposure ($\beta = .33$, $p < .01$), proportion of English use ($\beta = .26$, $p < .05$), and Spanish CALP ($\beta = .54$, $p < .001$). Spanish CALP appeared to be the strongest predictor in the model.

At the final step of the model, the SPM score representing nonverbal thinking/perceptual skills was entered. This variable was entered into the model because English CALP was the only outcome variable with which it demonstrated a statistically significant correlation. The model remained significant, $F(5, 73) = 9.45$, $p < .001$, and predicted a moderate 35% of the total variance (with $R^2 = .39$. and adjusted $R^2 = .35$) (Plonsky & Ghandar, 2018).

Table 6 Hierarchical regression predicting English CALP.

	English CALP		
	B	SE B	β
Step 1			
Age of Arrival	−.02	.14	−.01
Step 2			
Age of Arrival	.20	.15	.17
Early English Use	.72	.24	.38**
Step 3			
Age of Arrival	.24	.15	.20
Early English Use	.63	.24	.33**
Proportion English Use	10.37	5.86	.20
Step 4			
Age of Arrival	−.10	.15	−.08
Early English Use	.64	.21	.33**
Proportion English Use	13.30	5.20	.26*
Spanish CALP	.55	.12	.54***
Step 5			
Age of Arrival	−.03	.15	−.02
Early English Use	.70	.20	.36**
Proportion English Use	10.20	5.20	.20
Spanish CALP	.49	.11	.49**
SPM	.07	.03	.23*

Notes. Adjusted R^2 = .00, p = .91 for Step 1; R^2 Δ = .11, Adjusted R^2 = .09, $p < .05$ for Step 2;
R^2 Δ = .04, Adjusted R^2 = .11, $p < .01$ for Step 3; R^2 Δ = .20, Adjusted R^2 = .31, $p < .001$ for Step 4; R^2 Δ = .05, Adjusted R^2 = .35, $p < .001$ for Step 5.
*$p < .05$; **$p < .01$; ***$p < .001$; N = 78.

The 5% change in R^2 was significant, $F(1, 73) = 5.86, p < .05$. Within the final model, Spanish CALP ($\beta = .49, p < .001$) had a greater weight than SPM scores ($\beta = .23, p = < .05$) or English use ($\beta = .37, p = .001$) These results indicate that while early language exposure and nonverbal cognitive skills play roles in the acquisition of English CALP, Spanish-English bilingual speakers with the strongest Spanish CALP attain higher levels of English CALP. SPM, on the other hand, does not correlate significantly with Spanish CALP.

4.5.5 Research Question 5: Spanish CALP

The final model examined the relation of the other predictor variables to Spanish CALP (refer Table 5). Age of arrival was entered at Step 1, and resulted in a significant model, $F(1, 76) = 32.38, p < .001$. The model predicted 29% of the variance, a medium effect size (Cohen, 1988), with $R^2 = .30$ and adjusted $R^2 = .29$. At Step 2 of the model years of education in Spanish was entered. The model remained significant, $F(2, 75) = 16.27, p < .001$, but the R^2 change of 4.1% was not significant. The new model predicted 28% of the variance with $R^2 = .30$ and adjusted $R^2 = .28$. At the final step of the model proportion of Spanish use was added, resulting in a significant model, $F(3, 74) = 11.10$, $p < .001$, but no significant change in R^2. The model continued to predict 28% of the variance in Spanish CALP. In the final model, age of arrival was the only predictor that was significant ($\beta = .498, p < .001$). The model indicates that later arrivals will have better Spanish CALP skills but does not provide a potential explanation of factors resulting in a higher degree of Spanish CALP.

Post-hoc analysis of variance was utilized to explore differences between group means in Spanish CALP for two different grouping variables: amount of early Spanish exposure (as represented by years of Spanish education), and proportion of Spanish use for the past five years. Subjects were first divided into two groups based on fewer years of Spanish education (0–5): designated group 1 ($N = 53$), versus more years of Spanish education (6 or more), designated group 2 ($N = 26$). The mean Spanish CALP score for group 1 was 84.34 (SD 7.92) and the mean Spanish CALP score for group 2 was 90.23 (SD 6.94). The difference between group means was significant, $F(1, 77) = 10.45, p < .01$. Within-group variances for this analysis met the standard for Levene's test of homogeneity of variances.

Subjects were also partitioned into two groups based on proportion of Spanish use (in the past five years). Group 1 ($N = 49$) demonstrated a proportion of Spanish use of .49 or less, while group 2 ($N = 30$) reported using a proportion of Spanish of .5 or more. The mean score for group 1 was 85.31 (SD 8.08). The mean for group 2 was 88.20 (SD 7.35). The difference between group means was not significant, $F(1, 77) = 2.55, p = .11$.

Results from the series of post hoc ANOVAs suggest that individuals with greater degrees of early Spanish exposure are likely to achieve higher Spanish CALP levels. No significant difference in group means was noted based on differences in proportion of recent Spanish use.

5 What Are the Implications for SLA, Bilingualism, and Pedagogy?

5.1 The Interaction of the Predictor Variables with Bilingual Language Outcomes

The results of the current study challenge some popular assumptions about bilingualism. For example, younger L2 learners traditionally are perceived as having better learning outcomes in an L2. A further assumption is that "native-like" accent is equivalent to a high degree of overall language skill. Employing the BICS/CALP distinction in the study and utilizing a reliable test of CALP as a measuring stick against which to compare language outcomes permit differentiation among them in reference to the impact of the variables of interest. The results of the study also contribute to a more precise understanding of the constructs of BICS and CALP. Table 7 provides a summary of the relations of predictors to outcomes for the entire study.

5.1.1 Age of Arrival and Bilingual Language Skills

Outcomes from this study provide further evidence that age of arrival (a measure of AOA) has a significant effect on English (L2) accent. Age of arrival negatively predicted this skill, while level of Spanish or English CALP had no impact on competence. In other words, earlier arrivals are likely to demonstrate more "native-like" accent in English. This result is consistent with findings by Flege (1999) and Yeni-Komshian et al. (2000) and in line with the notion that phonology in L2 is subject to maturational constraints and a primary discourse ability that is mastered implicitly.

Similarly, production of English regular past tense verbs (an L2 grammatical skill) was also related to age of arrival. It is a skill that bears some resemblance to the skill of "native-like" accent, in that it requires the ability to accurately produce English speech sounds in a word-final position (as English past tense is marked via morphemes comprised of single phonemes (/t/, /d/), or the syllable /ɪd/). Again, these outcomes would be in line with an understanding of core grammar abilities as implicitly learned procedural knowledge subject to maturational constraints and a component of primary discourse abilities or BICS.

The current study found a notable lack of relationship between English (L2) CALP and age of arrival. Based on these results it appears there must be other factors besides early exposure to English that support the achievement of higher levels of cognitive and academic proficiency. These findings also indicate that accent and L2 CALP are very different types of language skills, predicted by different variables. Results indicate that it is conceivable that an individual with an early age of arrival and a highly rated accent could be disadvantaged in the acquisition of English (L2) CALP, depending on the combination of events (predictors) experienced by that person.

Age of arrival predicted the Spanish language skills of advanced verb production. Once Spanish CALP was taken into account in predicting advanced verb production, age of arrival was no longer significant. Spanish

Table 7 Predictors of bilingual language skills.

English Accent	English Regular Past Tense	English Irregular Past Tense	Spanish Advanced Verbs	English CALP	Spanish CALP
(−) Age of Arrival	(−) Age of Arrival**	(+) Early English Exposure			(+) Age of Arrival
	(+) Early English Exposure			(+) Early English Exposure	
(+) Proportion of English Use					
	(+) English CALP**	(+) Spanish CALP	(+) Spanish CALP	(+) Spanish CALP	
		(+) English CALP***			
				(+) SPM	

Notes. **Significant in post hoc analysis with English CALP substituted for Spanish CALP as a predictor in Step 4; ***Significant in post hoc analysis with English CALP added as a predictor.

CALP strongly predicted production of advanced verb forms. Although age of arrival dropped out of the model predicting advanced verbs, logically there must be a vehicle or vehicles for arriving at this advanced level of skill. Examination of group differences to explore this question found that later arrivals demonstrate greater ability in the production of advanced Spanish verb forms. These findings are consistent with observations from Montrul (1999) and Köpke (2004). It appears that later arrivals are less likely to experience L1 attrition than earlier arrivals. Köpke (2004) notes that higher L1 education levels seem to prevent attrition. It is likely, therefore, that later arrivals may have more years of education in Spanish. The link between L1 (Spanish) CALP and advanced verb production would support a view that places this grammatical skill within the realm of secondary discourse ability, not subject to maturational constraints. Advanced grammatical abilities would appear to be controlled to some degree by the metalinguistic skills located within the CUP.

Age of arrival was the only predictor found to be significant in predicting Spanish CALP (later arrivals demonstrated greater skill). Age of arrival did not predict English CALP. Apparently, age effects are different for L1 and L2 cognitive and academic language proficiencies. Early exposure to L2 does not appear to contribute in a significant fashion to the development of L2 CALP but is negatively related to the acquisition of L1 CALP.

5.1.2 Language Exposure/Use and Bilingual Language Skills

All English language outcomes except accent were predicted by early English exposure (as measured by number of years of education in the language). The results for accent approached significance. These results are logical, as language skills cannot emerge in a vacuum.

Regular past tense production was predicted in this study by early English exposure until strong English CALP subsumed the variance remaining from the entry of age of arrival. These findings are similar to those of White and Genesee (1996), who reported that greater use results in a higher degree of proficiency in L2 grammar. Flege et al. (1999) related proficiency in grammar to years of schooling in the United States, which in this study was equated to early language exposure. In viewing the role of early language exposure and use, it may be possible to see it as a bridge to CALP; this is further supported by the fact that use of irregular past tense verbs is predicted by early English exposure until English CALP is entered into the model. It is also notable that English CALP is also predicted by early English exposure.

Proportion of English use within the past five years significantly predicted English accent. The evidence that adult language use predicts these skills indicates that language use may overcome disadvantages secondary to age effects. Language use may be viewed as a bridge to specific language competencies even in domains thought to be wholly "reserved" for early language learners.

5.1.3 L1 Proficiency and L2 Acquisition

Spanish (L1) CALP positively predicted Spanish advanced verb production. It also predicted an English grammatical skill, irregular past tense production. The relation of English irregular past tense with Spanish CALP, as well as the lack of a significant relationship of L2 irregular past tense with age, differentiated irregular from regular past tense production. Characteristics of irregular past tense forms may assist in explaining the distinction. For example, irregular past tense forms appear less frequently in the English language than regular past tense forms (Nicoladis, Palmer, & Marentette, 2007) and have been associated with semantic knowledge (Patterson, Lambon Ralph, Hodges, & McClelland, 2001) and declarative memory (Ullman, 2001). The CALP measure employed in this study (the WMLS-NU) is a measure of semantic skill. Apparently, irregular past tense is related to semantic skill (as explicitly learned, and a probable secondary discourse ability) as measured by the WMLS-NU, whereas regular past tense appears more related to implicitly learned phonological skills (primary discourse abilities). If irregular past tense is related to semantic skill, then it appears that greater semantic skill in L1 leads to greater semantic skill in L2. This outcome appears logical in light of the study's current findings regarding Spanish CALP and English CALP.

English CALP was predicted by Spanish CALP. From the results of the current study it appears that CALP in L1 contributes significantly to CALP in L2. This would be consistent with arguments by Köpke (2004) and Francis (2012) stating that L2 acquisition is linked to the learner's previous linguistic knowledge level, making L1 as a primary resource for L2 learning. This finding also supports findings by Ramirez et al. (1991) and Jiang and Kuehn (2001) linking greater L1 skill to better academic outcomes in L2 (English). As previously noted, English CALP was not predicted by age of arrival.

5.2 A Chronological Model of Bilingual Language Skill Predictors

This study was designed to examine bilingual language skills and their emergence in a chronological model (relevant to the L2 acquisition timeline).

Spanish (L1) and English (L2) language skills were considered in parallel along a timeline. Moving across the timeline, the impacts of age of arrival, early language exposure (as represented by years of education in each language), and proportion of language use (in the last five years) of each language were evaluated. At the far endpoint (CALP attainment), the influence of L1 CALP on L2 CALP was assessed as the direction of this relationship would be logical in the (chronological) model. A summary of the findings is illustrated in Figure 1.

In general the model assumes that L1 skills provide the foundation for and impact L2 secondary discourse acquisition. In other words, the starting point for the language skill of a sequential bilingual speaker is the L1. Intervening variables (age of arrival, exposure, use) will either facilitate L1 skill development or contribute to attrition (Montrul, 2005). The model indicates that negative effects for L1 may limit attainment in L2 for some skills, specifically CALP and CALP-related abilities. For example, early age of arrival predicts lower attainment in L1 CALP, and L1 CALP predicts L2 CALP. Thus, lower L1 CALP due to early age of arrival can result in a delimiting of L2 CALP. By applying the logic of this model to the language skills of sequential bilingual speakers, some predictions can be made about the combinations of variables that will result in high degrees of BICS and CALP proficiency in both languages.

What combination of factors describes a highly proficient (in both languages) Spanish English *sequential* bilingual speaker? If BICS and CALP (primary/secondary discourse skills) are both considered, then the highly proficient bilingual individual will likely be an early arrival (thus a better L2 accent), who has six or more years of education provided in Spanish. This individual will have highly developed Spanish CALP (likely due to academic exposure to the language) and will eventually attain high levels of CALP in English over time.

Because AOA (age of arrival) has such a significant impact on Spanish CALP (with later arrivals performing better on the WMLS-NU), it is likely that those who arrive after the age of eight will attain greater Spanish CALP and therefore greater English CALP. Accent may be rated as less "native-like" than that of the early arrival, but other outcomes may exceed skill levels of the early arrival. The effects of earlier arrival may be ameliorated (in terms of impact on Spanish CALP) by an increase in early use of Spanish (more years of Spanish language education).

What happens in the case that L1 CALP fails to develop to a highly proficient level? A number of authors in the field of bilingual education have suggested that poor CALP development in L1, or language loss in L1, has resulted for

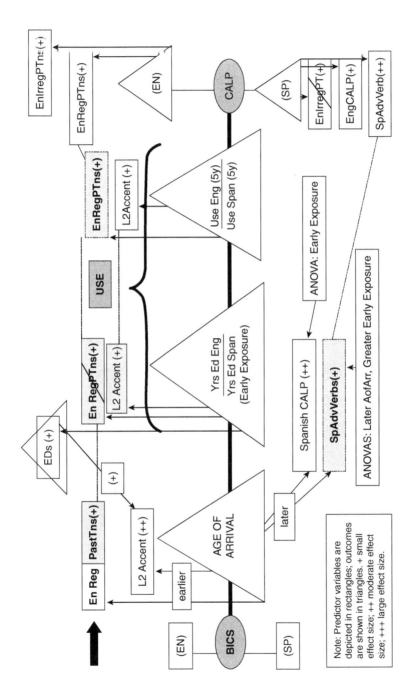

Figure 1. The effects of predictors on bilingual language skills: A chronological model.

many bilingual speakers in limited CALP attainment in L2 (English) and resulting academic difficulties (Baca & Cervantes, 1998; Valenzuela, 1999).

For Spanish-English bilingual speakers, then, a number of English (L2) outcomes appear to relate to level of attainment in L1 (Spanish) CALP, which in this study is the primary predictor of English CALP. In turn, English CALP predicts regular and irregular English past tense skill. Spanish CALP predicts English irregular past tense use and use of advanced Spanish grammatical forms as well. The question then becomes one of determining how a speaker attains a high degree of Spanish CALP, which appears to favorably affect a number of outcomes in L1 as well as in L2 (English). Examination of outcomes for Spanish CALP in a group of individuals with greater early exposure to/use of Spanish versus a group with less early exposure indicated those with greater early exposure (more years of Spanish education) demonstrated greater attainment of Spanish CALP.

5.3 Limitations of the Study

This study provides preliminary evidence for the effects of amount of language use in the acquisition of bilingual language skills. It has been acknowledged that the construct of language use or contact is difficult to measure consistently (Köpke, 2004; Köpke & Schmid, 2003). This difficulty was observed in the current study that asked participants to estimate language use in terms of percentages. Many appeared to struggle with delineating language use in such terms. A more refined measure than that used in the current study might yield more powerful results. Furthermore, the variable of years of education in each language was selected as a measure of early language exposure for this study. The issue of early language use in the home was not addressed, and it is assumed that such use is highly significant in bilingual language acquisition.

In considering years of education as a variable, lack of equivalency of types of "Spanish language education" is acknowledged. For example, in the United States most L1 education for non-English speakers is provided in bilingual classrooms in which English is also taught. Therefore, talking time is shared between L1 and English. On the other hand, years of Spanish language educa-tion occurring in another country are likely to be all in Spanish. More precise disaggregating of the data to differentiate between these categories of early L1 use would possibly add explanatory power to the models. However, this study provides strong evidence that childhood use of both languages supports skills in both languages.

This study's design has some inherent limitations; for example, it is acknowledged that there are aspects of language proficiency that are not measured by the WMLS-NU. Some of these factors may also be impacted by the variables in question. For example, overall comprehension skills were not addressed in this study even though they are considered in some measures of language proficiency. It is also acknowledged that social and motivation factors have a strong impact on L2 acquisition and L1 maintenance. However, the impact of these was not covered by this particular design. Finally, the sample for this study (college-educated bilingual speakers) likely limits its generalizability.

5.4 Directions for Further Research

Future research is needed to assess the probability of positive transfer of skills from L2 (English) to L1 (Spanish), a phenomenon that has received some attention in the literature in studies of literacy skills. Durgunoğlu, Nagy, and Hancin-Bhatt (1993) provided early evidence of transfer of phonological awareness abilities. Cárdenas-Hagan, Carlson, and Pollard-Durodola (2007) give an updated review and exploration of the topic with similar results for a number of preliteracy and early literacy skills. Other skill areas should be examined in the same light. Transfer effects from English to Spanish CALP are particularly interesting in light of the current study. Such studies could take into account the notion that there may be a threshold of L1 CALP develop-ment. The "threshold hypothesis" (Cummins, 1981) indicates that when such a level is reached it may provide the necessary support for attaining high degrees of L2 CALP development. The question arises as to whether this can occur without accompanying L1 CALP growth, an area that has not been systematically explored. This springboard relation of L1 CALP to L2 CALP is suggested in the data collected for this study in that the mean scores for English CALP approached one SD above the mean scores for Spanish CALP. Studies with developing bilingual children would provide "real-time" evidence for how L1 and L2 CALP impact each other during language development stages.

Another research question emerging from this study relates to potential differences between the impacts of age of arrival and reported age of L2 acquisition on different language skills. According to the data collected for the current study, these two demonstrate a moderately strong correlation but are different variables (Hernandez & Li, 2007). It would be informative to compare the effects of the two different predictors on the same language outcomes.

In summary, the current study provides confirmation regarding the impact of significant variables on bilingual language outcomes, assessed concurrently. The study also provides new information regarding the places of L2 accent, L1 and L2 grammatical skills, and L2 CALP on the continuum of BICS versus CALP. While the role of language use, highlighted as problematic from a measurement standpoint, continues to be difficult to consistently define, the study permits the linking of BICS and CALP skills to variables of age and use to determine the role these predictors play in attaining high degrees of competency in the target skills.

5.5 Theoretical Frameworks for the Interpretation of Results

A variety of theoretical frameworks have been utilized to conceptualize the language proficiencies of bilingual or multilingual speakers and the roles of the variables emphasized above. A comprehensive discussion of these frameworks is outside the scope of this Element; however, the authors consider that two in particular have strong explanatory power for outcomes in the present study (and the resultant model): usage-based theory and dynamic systems theory.

Usage-based theory (UBT) emphasizes that humans develop their language systems in contexts where language is used; linguistic skills in each language arise as speakers have experience and opportunity to use a language:

> The linguistic skills that a person possesses at any given moment in time – in the form of a "structured inventory of symbolic units" – result from her accumulated experience with language across the totality of usage events in her life. This accumulated linguistic experience undergoes processes of entrenchment, due to repeated uses of particular expressions across usage events, and abstraction, due to type variation in constituents of particular expressions across usage events. (Tomasello, 2000, pp. 61–2)

Sequential bilingual (or multilingual) speakers experience changes in context and code as they engage in usage events, and function, in different language settings. Depending on those settings, the "totality of usage events" may happen in L1, L2, or a combination of language settings. The linguistic skills that result from those language experiences reflect those usage events.

As bilingual children spend more or less time using their different languages based on the contexts in which they listen and speak, their language productions change. Language abilities may be gained or lost depending on degree of usage. Theorists note a maturational effect on L1 attrition, with younger speakers experiencing more L1 attrition when exposure to that language is limited.

Usage of language impacts L2 proficiency, as observed in the current study. Age effects are noted for aspects of L2 acquisition, but variations in usage of L2 appear to play a more significant role in L2 acquisition than age. Limitations in usage result in variations in language products for bilingual speakers (in comparison to expectations for monolingual speakers). In this study, early usage, as measured by degree of early exposure to L2, predicted a number of L2 outcomes (English regular and irregular past tense marking, English CALP level). On the other hand, current degree of use of L2 (English) positively predicted only the degree to which speakers were perceived to have a native-like accent.

The impact of early exposure and use of L1 was not clearly evidenced in the results of this study (although results of the post hoc ANOVA did suggest that participants with greater early exposure to L1 have stronger proficiency). An explanation for these results is believed to lie in the measurement of L1 use, particularly for early exposure and usage. The measure used in this study for early exposure/usage of L1 and L2 was number of years of schooling in each language. This measure appeared effective for assessing L2 exposure, which is typically more limited than L1 exposure in childhood. However, as L1 is the language of the home for most sequential bilingual speakers, number of years of schooling in L1 appeared to fail to sufficiently encompass actual L1 exposure. The variable "age of arrival," on the other hand, was a strong, and singular, positive predictor of Spanish CALP in the primary analysis (older arrivals had higher Spanish CALP levels). It is logical to view age of arrival as a (negative) predictor of early exposure and use of L1; arrival to the new context where L2 is introduced necessarily means the beginning of reduced exposure to/usage of L1. Interestingly, age of arrival was not a predictor of advanced Spanish verb usage; this is considered in the discussion that follows.

A relevant question at this point emerging from the current study (and connected to maturational effects on attrition) is regarding the potential ameliorating impact of high levels of cognitive/academic language proficiency on decreased usage in L1 (and potentially L2). Once a sufficient level of language abstraction is achieved (as reflected by CALP measures), does decreased usage have a limited impact on specific language abilities? Our results would support this generalization, as amount of current use did not predict language outcomes in L1 (Spanish) or L2 (English) for highly proficient adult bilinguals in any area other than L2 (English) accent.[3] The idea that a high degree of CALP, particularly in L1, can offset the effects of decreased usage of the language could also correlate with observed maturational effects noted for attrition, with

---

[3] Support for the notion that use/exposure does not explain L1 proficiency is found in Schmid and Köpke (2018a), who in their review of relevant literature specific to usage and L1 attrition note that "the absence of an effect of exposure, and in particular of the frequency of use in informal contexts, has since been replicated across a host of investigations of attrition across a range of linguistic levels" (p. 656).

older L2 learners (seen in this study to be more likely to attain high L1 CALP levels) being less likely to demonstrate L1 loss.

The fact that the language skills of bilingual speakers respond to frequently changing language environments points to the relevance of dynamic systems theory (DST) for understanding the proposed chronological model of sequential bilingual language acquisition. Rosmawati (2014) provides a general summary of dynamic systems theory as follows: "DST is a theory of how change happens over time ... and how it shapes the outward behaviour of the system. In other words, it is a theory of how development unfolds" (p. 67). A number of scholars, beginning with de Bot et al. (2007), have connected DST with bilingualism and L2 acquisition. In line with what has already been noted, bilinguals' exposure to and opportunity to develop/acquire/use each of their languages change over time (as they acquire language in dynamic, changing environments). Specific language abilities, which emerge from the complex and dynamic linguistic system, change accordingly (Schmid & Köpke, 2018b; Schmid et al., 2013,). DST allows for the conceptualization that bilingual language skills are modifiable (in positive and "negative" senses) and that this is typical for bilingual speakers. A similar type of conceptualization has been proposed by Hernandez and colleagues (Hernandez, 2013; Hernandez & Li, 2007; Hernandez, Li, & Macwhinney, 2005; Hernandez et al., 2019a) using an Emergentists framework. Li and colleagues connect the DST perspective to the structural neuroplasticity noted for neural changes related to dynamic L2 experience (Li et al., 2014).

Kohnert (2013) also notes the interplay between dynamic language environments, changing patterns of usage, and variations in language abilities. She folds insights from UBT and DST, along with knowledge developed from neurobiological research, into a definition of language as "a dynamical system that emerges within a social context through interactions of cognitive, neurobiological and environmental systems and subsystems across nested timescales," and denotes it as a "Dynamic Interactive Processing Perspective (DIPP)" (p. 14). This Neuroemergentist perspective captures the influences of dynamic, changing language environments which impact the bilingual language system and its use across varying ages and individual ability levels, with varying degrees of impact on different language products and skills. This understanding stands in contrast to views of language abilities as, once acquired, fixed and settled. Learnings gained from these perspectives thus permit an explanation of language attrition, for example, as part of a normal phenomenon versus an indication of a language deficit.

The chronological model proposed in this Element fits well within this framework as it addresses changing language environments of bilingual speakers over time (assessing exposure and use) in seeking to account for differences in primary and secondary discourse abilities in varying AOAs. Again, by acknowledging and explaining the multitude of factors which influence bilingual language proficiencies at any given point in time, the DIPP is a "unifying conceptualization of language" (p. 13) which permits observers to make hypotheses about bilingual language skills outside of expectations drawn from monolingual language behaviors.

5.6 Implications for Bilingual Families and Educators

An important implication of this research lies in the support that it provides for the development of L1 CALP for sequential bilingual speakers, and therefore to strong bilingual education programs. In addition to being significant for its own sake, L1 (Spanish) CALP is a primary predictor of L2 CALP. These results would appear to provide support for Cummin's (1981) linguistic interdependence hypothesis, indicating that many skills in a well-developed L1 transfer and support the learning of an L2, again substantiating Francis' (2012) description of L1 as a primary L2 resource. A related generalization from the current study would be that sequential bilingual speakers must use the language in which they start their lives as communicating beings (their L1) to gain early cognitive/domain-general abilities, which then permit or constrain acquisition of high-level L2 skills. This connects to Cummins' (1976) "threshold hypothesis," which indicates that a threshold level of L1 competence must be attained by a sequential bilingual speaker in order to realize cognitive advantages from bilingualism.

One aspect of bilingualism that was not fully addressed in this study was the effect of language typology and the particular interaction between English and Spanish. Recent work by Hartshorne et al. (2018) has found different windows during which L2 acquisition results in a more optimal outcome. For Chinese, the optimal window is 6–10 years of age, whereas for Romance languages it was at 0. For west Germanic languages the optimal age was between 1 and 5. English has a considerable influence on both its lexical and syntactic structure due to the influx of Latin-based words. For example, Ambridge and colleagues (2014) found that monolingual English-speaking adults but not children had awareness of verbs that came from Latin. These particular verbs will use the "to ... " construction to indicate a dative which is borrowed directly from the syntax used in Romance languages. In a similar vein, morphological awareness is enhanced when monolingual English-speaking children are placed into dual-language immersion programs relative to those in single-language classrooms (Kuo, Ramirez, de Marin, Kim, & Unal-Gezer, 2017). This shows that CALP in English may actually be more influenced by Romance language knowledge than other languages. Future studies are needed to flesh this out more completely.

At least in terms of the language skills deemed important to academic success (when academic programming is provided in L2), early exposure to the L2 is not necessarily key. It appears to be more significant for L2 success that the sequential bilingual language learner first has the opportunity to develop linguistic competence in L1. The current outcomes support more and higher quality bilingual education programs, for example, in which the focus is not only on acquisition of English but on attainment of greater L1 CALP, or secondary discourse skills, as well.

5.7 Implications for Language Assessment and Diagnosis of Language Disorders

Another important application of this research lies in the area of developmental evaluation of language skills; this study provides evidence that bilinguals may differ on some skills from monolinguals, depending on how language skills are impacted by the variables discussed here. For example, an eight-year-old child who is an early arrival, and who does not receive education in Spanish, may not demonstrate use of advanced Spanish verb forms (although use of these would be expected according to normative information for monolingual Spanish speakers.) What is "typical" in Spanish and in English for a bilingual speaker appears to differ from what is "typical" in each language for a monolingual speaker. This must be taken into account when language is being evaluated for the purpose of determining whether or not a language delay or impairment may be present.

Given the highly varied language characteristics of bilingual speakers, it would be more productive to invest assessment time and resources in evaluating the abilities within the common underlying proficiency, or central operating system, that serves both languages. Such assessment strategies are beyond the scope of this Element, but a number of authors provide a thorough discussion of means of assessing domain-general skills underlying language abilities (see Kohnert, 2013, for a discussion of process measures and other alternative assessment strategies that are "aimed at assessing the integrity of the system used in the service of language," p. 169).

6 Conclusion: Moving Away from a Deficiency View of Bilingual Language Skills

A related implication, then, based on the perspective taken in this Element, is the importance of moving away from a "deficit view" of the primary discourse abilities of sequential bilingual speakers. The terminology consistently utilized across the disciplines of bilingualism and L2 acquisition reflects a "less than" perspective on the specific language skills (phonology, grammar, syntax) of bilingual speakers. For example, the terms "incomplete," "attrition," "loss," "erosion," and "errors" are typically employed in studies focusing on the specific language products emerging from bilinguals' different language systems. Moving forward in understanding bilingual language acquisition would indicate that new terminology is needed. Hernandez and colleagues (2019b) have taken on this view when considering the language attrition literature. For child learners, they suggest the term "language absorption," which reveals not a loss but a process of it being reconstituted for another purpose. For adult learners, they propose "language reconfiguration," which fits in with the notion of adapting existing knowledge to fit in with new needs. These terms reflect a sense of what is typical, and expected, for bilingual speakers in dynamic contexts.

As we consider the interactions of the many factors that feed language development and language acquisition in these speakers, it is clear that there is (inevitably) incredible individual variation. Rather than viewing variations in accent, grammar, and lexicon as reflections of language abilities that are "less than" those of a monolingual speaker, these variations should be viewed as reflecting an expected range of characteristics for bilingual speakers of given languages. Sanchez (2018) clearly summarizes this perspective:

> Attriters and heritage speakers are part of the continuum of bilingualism that ranges from bilinguals with sustained lexical access and activation in both languages to bilinguals with limited access and activation . . . These different levels of access can be incorporated into a single model for bilinguals across the continuum. (p. 755)

Understanding bilingualism, or multilingualism, as a continuum makes space for all the rich variation that is exhibited in a dynamic world of communicators.

Appendix A

Language Background Questionnaire (Adapted from Flege & MacKay, 2004)

The purpose of this questionnaire is to learn something about your language history. We would like to find out what languages you know, when you first learned them, and how much you use them.

1. Gender:
2. Today's Date:
3. Place of birth:
4. Date of Birth:
5. What is your first language? _____ 2nd _____ 3rd

   _____

6. How old were you when you began to learn/speak Spanish? _____
   English?_____
7. How did you learn Spanish? _____ English?

   _____

8. If born in another country, age of arrival to the US:

   _____

9. Years and places you have lived other than in the US:

   _____

10. Did you receive any education in Spanish?

    _____

11. If so, how many years of formal education in Spanish did you have?

    _____

12. How many years of formal education in English did you have?

    _____

13. How many years education did your father complete? _____Your
    mother?_____

Please estimate to the nearest 10% how much you speak any kind of **Spanish** in these places and situations. Try to base your estimate on your use of **Spanish** over the past 5 years

	0%	10%	20%	30%	40%	50%	60%	70%	80%	90%	100%
At home											
In college classes											
Visiting family members											
At work (including volunteer work)											
Church/church functions											
On the telephone											
On vacation											
While shopping											
At parties and social gatherings											
Visiting friends											

Please estimate, using a percentage (%), how much you have spoken **Spanish**:

Past 10 years _____ ; Past 5 years _____ ; Past 5 months _____ ; Past 5 weeks _____

Please estimate to the nearest 10% how much you speak any kind of **English** in these places and situations. Try to base your estimate on your use of **English** over the past 5 years

	0%	10%	20%	30%	40%	50%	60%	70%	80%	90%	100%
At home											
In college classes											
Visiting family members											
At work (including volunteer work)											
Church/church functions											
On the telephone											
On vacation											
While shopping											
At parties and social gatherings											
Visiting friends											

Please estimate, using a percentage (%), how much you have spoken **English**:

Past 10 years _____ ; Past 5 years _____ ; Past 5 months _____ ; Past 5 weeks _____

Please estimate your ability to speak, understand, read, and write English and Spanish. Use the number "1" if you feel your ability is very limited, use the number "7" if your ability is excellent, and numbers in between for ability levels that are in between.

English	1	2	3	4	5	6	7	Spanish	1	2	3	4	5	6	7
Speaking								***							
Understanding								***							
Reading								***							
Writing								***							

CURRENTLY: How many hours per day (estimate) do you speak ENGLISH? _____

How many hours per day (estimate) do you speak SPANISH? _____

Appendix B
Accent Rating Paragraph

The following paragraph was taken from the Speech Accent Archive website (http://accent.gmu.edu/). Read the following paragraph silently to yourself; you will have one minute to do so. Then you will read the paragraph aloud for taping. Just read it as you normally would read aloud.

> Please call Stella. Ask her to bring these things with her from the store: Six spoons of fresh snow peas, five thick slabs of blue cheese, and maybe a snack for her brother Bob. We also need a small plastic snake and a big toy frog for the kids. She can scoop these things into three red bags, and we will go meet her Wednesday at the train station.

Appendix C

English Past Tense Production Test (Items Administered in Random Order)

1. blame	[d]		21. guess	[t]	
2. gain	[d]		22. place	[t]	
3. name	[d]		23. hope	[t]	
4. love	[d]		24. like	[t]	
5. solve	[d]		25. pop	[t]	
6. beg	[d]		26. mix	[t]	
7. rob	[d]		27. switch	[t]	
8. train	[d]		28. check	[t]	
9. save	[d]		29. shock	[t]	
10. groan	[d]		30. reach	[t]	
11. fill	[d]		31. face	[t]	
12. kill	[d]		32. chop	[t]	
13. file	[d]		33. crush	[t]	
14. sail	[d]		34. wrap	[t]	
15. crawl	[d]		35. bake	[t]	
16. frown	[d]		36. smoke	[t]	
17. bowl	[d]		37. splash	[t]	
18. wave	[d]		38. chase	[t]	
19. breathe	[d]		39. blink	[t]	
20. plunge	[d]		40. slap	[t]	

Column Total Correct: _____   Column Total Correct: _____

41. grant	[id]	61. wear	[wore]
42. hate	[id]	62. break	[broke]
43. head	[id]	63. run	[ran]
44. tend	[id]	64. sit	[sat]
45. tempt	[id]	65. grow	[grew]
46. fade	[id]	66. know	[knew]
47. treat	[id]	67. draw	[drew]
48. rent	[id]	68. see	[saw]
49. lift	[id]	69. take	[took]
50. wait	[id]	70. shake	[shook]
51. shout	[id]	71. find	[found]
52. melt	[id]	72. rise	[rose]
53. pat	[id]	73. write	[wrote]
54. float	[id]	74. drive	[drove]
55. greet	[id]	75. fall	[fell]
56. hunt	[id]	76. hold	[held]
57. chat	[id]	77. come	[came]
58. wound	[id]	78. give	[gave]
59. twist	[id]	79. stand	[stood]
60. plant	[id]	80. go	[went]

Column Total Correct:_____ /Reg PT (1–60) Correct:_____ Column/Irr PT (61–80) Total Correct:_____

Appendix D

Spanish Verb Test

A continuación escucharas un verbo. Utilízalo al final de la oración que te daremos.

Verbs: 10; Early forms (regular 1st/3rd person present/preterit) (Target response in parentheses)

1. Escribir	1. La niña estaba escribiendo una carta. Ésta es la carta que ella (escribió)
2. Comprar	2. La mamá estaba comprando comida. Ésta es la carne que ella (compró)
3. Escuchar	3. El niño estaba escuchando música. Éste es el CD que él (escuchó)
4. Ver	4. El papá estaba viendo un programa. El partido fue lo que él (vio)
5. Vivir	5. El médico no pensó que la mujer pudo vivir, pero le operó y ella sí (vivió)
6. Aprender	6. Quiero aprender este material, pero si no estudio entonces no lo (aprendo)
7. Comer	7. Tengo que comer pronto, me duele la cabeza si no (como)
8. Quedar	8. Si tú me invitas a quedar entonces me (quedo)
9. Hablar	9. Mi hermano no me escucha cuando yo le (hablo)
10. Entender	10. No puedo hacer esta tarea difícil porque no la (entiendo)

Total: _____

10 H/; Early forms (irregular 1st/3rd person present/preterit)

11. Dar	11. Yo quería que mi papá me diera un carro, pero una bicicleta es lo que me (dio)
12. Ir	12. Mi mamá se tenía que ir, entonces agarró su bolsa y (se fue)
13. Hacer	13. Yo no lo quería hacer, entonces mi hermano lo (hizo)
14. Tener	14. Yo pensé que papa tenía mis llaves, pero ayer el me dijo que nunca las (tuvo)
15. Venir	15. Le invité a mi amiga a mi casa anoche pero no (vino)
16. Poder	16. Si tú no puedes ir al teatro yo sí (puedo)
17. Estar	17. Mi mamá no está pero yo sí (estoy)
18. Saber	18. Mi hermano no sabe dónde está la llave pero yo sí lo (sé)
19. Ser	19. Yo soy Anna, ¿Y tú quién (eres)?
20. Oír	20. Yo no sé cómo me puedes oír porque hay mucho ruido y yo no te (oigo)

Total: _____

Total Score: Early Forms: _____

A continuación escucharas un verbo. Utilízalo al final de la oración que te daremos.

Verbs: 10; Advanced forms (regular 1st/3rd person subj/cond)

21. Escribir   21. No le escribí a mi abuela. Ella quería que yo le (escribiera) _____

22. Comprar   22. Mi mamá no me compró los dulces. Yo quería que me los (comprara) _____

23. Escuchar   23. El niño no quiso escuchar lo que dijo la maestra, pero ella quería que le (escuchara) _____

24. Ver   24. Yo no vi esa película. Mi amiga quería que la (viera) _____

25. Vivir   25. Cuando yo vivía en algunos lugares muy lejanos
mi prima siempre me venía a visitar; no importa por donde (viviera) _____

26. Aprender   26. Quiero aprender esa canción. Si me la pudieras enseñar, sé que la (aprendería) _____

27. Comer   27. No como la carne porque no me gusta. Si me gustara, entonces sí la (comería) _____

28. Quedar   28. Si me invitaras a quedar, entonces yo me (quedaría) _____

29. Hablar   29. Mi hermano no me escucha. Si él me escuchara, entonces yo le (hablaría) _____

30. Entender   30. No entiendo esta tarea. Si la maestra me la explicara, entonces la (entendería) _____

Total: _____

10; Advanced forms (irregular)

31. Dar   31. Yo quería darle el dinero, pero ella no quería que se lo (diera) _____

32. Ir   32. Ella siempre llevaba su pasaporte, no importa por donde (fuera) _____

33. Hacer   33. Yo no quería hacer el trabajo, pero mi mamá quería que lo (hiciera) _____

34. Tener   34. No tengo el dinero. Yo te daría el dinero si lo (tuviera) _____

35. Venir   35. Yo no quería venir a la fiesta hoy pero mi amiga quería que (viniera) _____

36. Poder   36. No puedo ir esta noche. Yo iría a la fiesta si (pudiera) _____

37. Decir   37. Si supiera la verdad, yo te la (diría) _____

38. Hacer   38. Si quisieras que hiciera tu tarea yo la (haría) _____

39. Dar   39. Si tuviera el dinero, te lo (daría) _____

40. Venir   40. Cuando lo invité a mi casa, Miguel dijo que tenía que trabajar. Si no tuviera que
trabajar, entonces el (vendría) _____

Total: _____

Total Score: Advanced Forms: _____

References

Abutalebi, J., & Green, D. (2007). Bilingual language production: The neuro-cognition of language representation and control. *Journal of Neurolinguistics, 20*(3), 242–75.

Adesope, O., Lavin, T., Thompson, T., & Ungerleider, C. (2010). A systematic review and meta-analysis of the cognitive correlates of bilingualism. *Review of Educational Research, 80*(2), 207–45.

Ambridge, B., Pine, J., Rowland, C., Freudenthal, D., & Chang, F. (2014). Avoiding dative overgeneralisation errors: Semantics, statistics, or both? *Language, Cognition, and Neuroscience, 29*(2), 218–43.

Anderson, R. (1999). Impact of first language loss on grammar in a bilingual child. *Communication Disorders Quarterly, 21*, 4–16.

Anderson, R. (2001). Lexical morphology and verb use in child first language loss: A preliminary case study investigation. *International Journal of Bilingualism, 5*(4), 377–401.

Anderson, R. (2004). First language loss in Spanish speaking children: Patterns of loss and implications for clinical practice. In B. Goldstein (ed.), *Bilingual Language Development and Disorders in Spanish-English Speakers* (pp. 53–76). Baltimore, MD: Brookes.

Archila-Suerte, P., Zevin, J., Bunta, F., & Hernandez, A. E. (2012). Age of acquisition and proficiency in a second language independently influence the perception of non-native speech. *Bilingualism: Language and Cognition, 15*(1), 190–201.

Archila-Suerte, P., Zevin, J., & Hernandez, A. E. (2015). The effect of age of acquisition, socioeducational status, and proficiency on the neural processing of second language speech sounds. *Brain and Language, 141*, 35–49.

Ardasheva, Y. (2016). A structural equation modeling investigation of relationships among school-aged ELs' individual difference characteristics and academic and second language outcomes. *Learning and Individual Differences, 47*, 194–206.

Baca, L., & Cervantes, H. (1998). *The Bilingual Special Education Interface.* Columbus, OH: Merrill.

Baker, C. (2006). *Foundations of Bilingual Education and Bilingualism*, 4th edn. Clevedon, UK: Multilingual Matters.

Baus, C., Costa, A., & Carreiras, M. (2013). On the effects of second language immersion on first language production. *Acta Psychologica, 142*(3), 402–9.

Bialystok, E., & Hakuta, K. (1999). Confounded age: Linguistic and cognitive factors in age differences for second language acquisition. In D. Birdsong (Ed.), *Second Language Acquisition and the Critical Period Hypothesis* (pp. 1–22). Mahwah, NJ: Erlbaum.

Bialystok, E., & Miller, B. (1999). The problem of age in second-language acquisition: Influences from language, structure and task. *Bilingualism: Language and Cognition, 2*, 127–45.

Bird, H., Ralph, M. A. Lambon, Seidenberg, M. S., McClelland, J. I., & Patterson, K. (2003) Deficits in phonology and past tense morphology. *Journal of Memory and Language, 48*, 502–26

Birdsong, D. (1999). Introduction: Whys and why nots of the Critical Period Hypothesis for second language acquisition. In D. Birdsong (Ed.), *Second Language Acquisition and the Critical Period Hypothesis* (pp. 1–22). Mahwah, NJ: Erlbaum.

Bohman, T., Bedore, L., Peña, E., Mendez-Perez, A., & Gillam, R. (2010). What you hear and what you say: Language performance in Spanish-English bilinguals. *International Journal of Bilingual Education and Bilingualism, 13*(3), 325–44.

Bongaerts, T. (1999). Ultimate attainment in L2 pronunciation: The case of very advanced late L2 learners. In D. Birdsong (Ed.), *Second Language Acquisition and the Critical Period Hypothesis* (pp. 133–59). Mahwah, NJ: Erlbaum.

Brenchley, J., & Brenchley, S. (2006). *Los cien verbos mas usados in el Español* [*The 100 most frequently used verbs in Spanish*]. Retrieved on October 6, 2009, from http://www.lingolex.com/comveren.htm.

Bylund, E. (2009). Maturational constraints and first language attrition. *Language Learning, 59*(3), 687–715.

Bylund, E. (2018). Interpreting age effects in language acquisition and attrition. *Linguistic Approaches to Bilingualism, 7*(6), 682–5.

Bylund, J. (2011). Thought and second language: A Vygotskian framework for understanding BICS and CALP. *Communique, 39*(5), 4–6.

Cárdenas-Hagan, E., Carlson, C., & Pollard-Durodola, S. (2007). The cross-linguistic transfer of early literacy skills: The role of initial L1 and L2 skills and language of instruction. *Language, Speech, and Hearing Services in School, 38*(3), 249–59.

Catani, M., Jones, D., & Ffytche, D. (2005). Perisylvian language networks of the human brain. *Annals of Neurology, 57* (1), 8–16.

Centeno, J., & Cairns, H. (2010). Assessing frequency effects on verb inflection use by Spanish-speaking individuals with agrammatism: Theoretical and clinical implications. *International Journal of Speech-Language Pathology, 12*(1), 35–46.

Chee, M., Tan, E., & Thiel, T. (1999). Mandarin and English single word processing studied with functional magnetic resonance imaging. *Journal of Neuroscience, 19*, 3050–6.

Cohen, J. (1988). *Statistical Power Analysis for the Behavioral Sciences*, 2nd edn. Hillsdale, NJ: Erlbaum.

Consonni, M., Cafiero, R., Marin, D., Tettamanti, M., Iadanza, A., Fabbro, F., & Perani, D. (2013). Neural convergence for language comprehension and grammatical class production in highly proficient bilinguals is independent of age of acquisition. *Cortex, 49*(5), 1252–8.

Cummins, J. (1976). The influence of bilingualism on cognitive growth: A synthesis of research findings and explanatory hypotheses. *Working Papers in Bilingualism, 9*, 1–43.

Cummins, J. (1981). The role of primary language development in promoting educational success for language minority students. Bilingual Education Office (Ed.), *Schooling and Language-Minority Students: A Theoretical Framework* (pp. 3–47). Los Angeles, CA: Evaluation, Dissemination and Assessment Center, California State University.

Cummins, J. (1983). Language proficiency in academic achievement. In J. Oller (Ed.), *Issues in Language Testing Research* (pp. 108–30). Rowley, MA: Newbury House.

Cummins, J. (1991). Interdependence of first- and second-language proficiency in bilingual children. In E. Bialystok (Ed.), *Language Processing in Bilingual Children* (pp. 70–89). Cambridge, England: Cambridge University Press.

Cummins, J. (2008). BICS and CALP: Empirical and theoretical status of the distinction. In A. Creese, P. Martin, & N. Hornberger (Eds.), *Ecology of Language* (pp. 487–99). New York, NY: Springer.

Cutler, A., Mehler, J., Norris, D., & Segui, J. (1989). Limits on bilingualism. *Nature, 340*, 229–30.

De Bot, K. (2018). One theory for acquisition and attrition? *Linguistic Approaches to Bilingualism, 7*(6),678–81.

De Bot, K., Lowie, W., & Verspoor, M. (2007). A Dynamic Systems Theory approach to second language acquisition. *Bilingualism: Language and Cognition, 10*(01), 7–21.

de Leeuw, E., Tusha, A., & Schmid, M. (2018). Individual phonological attrition in Albanian-English late bilinguals. *Bilingualism: Language and Cognition, 21*(2), 278–95.

DeKeyser, R., Alfi-Shabtay, I., & Dorit, R. (2010). Cross-linguistic evidence for the nature of age effects in second language acquisition. *Applied Psycholinguistics, 31*(3), 413–38.

Delcenserie, A., & Genesee, F. (2017). The effects of age of acquisition on verbal memory in bilinguals. *International Journal of Bilingualism*, *21*(5), 600–16.

Domínguez, L. (2013). *Understanding Interfaces: Second Language Acquisition and First Language Attrition of Spanish Subject Realization and Word Order Variation*. Amsterdam, The Netherlands/Philadelphia, PA: Benjamins.

Domínguez, L. (2018). Bridging the gap between selective and non-selective L1 attrition. The role of L1-L2 structural (dis)similarity. *Linguistic Approaches to Bilingualism*, *7*(6), 686–90.

Donnelly, S., Brooks, P., & Homer, B. (2015). Examining the bilingual advantage on conflict resolution tasks: A meta-analysis. In D. Noelle, R. Dale, A. Warlaumont, J. Yoshimi, T. Matlock, C. Jennings, & P. Maglio (Eds.), *Proceedings of the 37th Annual Meeting of the Cognitive Science Society* (pp. 596–601). Austin, TX: Cognitive Science Society.

Ducharme, J. (2018): Why kids learn languages more easily than you do. *Time*, *191*(20), 24.

Durgunoğlu, A., Nagy, W., & Hancin-Bhatt, B. (1993). Cross-language transfer of phonological awareness. *Journal of Educational Psychology*, *85*(3), 453–65.

Elman, J. (1993). Learning and development in neural networks: The importance of starting small. *Cognition*, *48*(1), 71–99.

Eubank, L., & Gregg, K. (1999). Critical periods and (second) language acquisition: Divide et impera. In D. Birdsong (Ed.), *Second Language Acquisition and the Critical Period Hypothesis* (pp. 65–99). Mahwah, NJ: Erlbaum.

Flege, J. (1999). Age of learning and second language speech. In D. Birdsong (Ed.), *Second Language Acquisition and the Critical Period Hypothesis*, (pp. 101–32). Mahwah, NJ: Erlbaum.

Flege, J., & McKay, I. (2004). Perceiving vowels in a second language. *Studies in Second Language Acquisition*, *26*, 1–34.

Flege, J., Yeni-Komshian, G., & Liu, S. (1999). Age constraints on second-language acquisition. *Journal of Memory & Language*, *41*, 78–104.

Francis, N. (2012). *Bilingual Competence and Bilingual Proficiency in Child Development*. Cambridge, MA: MIT Press.

Friedman, H., & Amoo, T. (1999). Rating the rating scales. *Journal of Marketing Management*, *9*, 114–23.

Gallego, M., & Marks, E. (2015). Frequency of subjunctive use in oral production in two varieties of Spanish. *Procedia-Social and Behavioral Sciences*, *173*, 162–7.

Ganan, B., Hauser, G., & Thomas, T. (2015). A correlational study investigating the relationship between the Fluidez en La Lectura Oral Lectura (IDEL FLO) and the English portion of the Illinois Standard Achievement Test (ISAT). *Procedia-Social and Behavioral Sciences, 197,* 2411–16.

Goldstein, B. (2000). *Cultural and Linguistic Diversity Resource Guide for Speech Language Pathologists.* San Diego, CA: Singular.

Grant, A., Dennis, N., & Li, P. (2014). Cognitive control, cognitive reserve, and memory in the aging bilingual brain. *Frontiers in Psychology, 5,* 1401.

Grady, C., Luk, G., Craik, F., & Bialystok, E. (2015). Brain network activity in monolingual and bilingual older adults. *Neuropsychologia, 66,* 170–81.

Grosjean, F. (1989). Neurolinguists, beware! The bilingual is not two monolinguals in one person. *Brain and language, 36*(1), 3–15.

Grundy, J., Anderson, J., & Bialystok, E. (2017). Neural correlates of cognitive processing in monolinguals and bilinguals. *Annals of the New York Academic of Sciences, 1396*(1), 183–201.

Grundy, J., & Timmer, K. (2017). Bilingualism and working memory capacity: A comprehensive meta-analysis. *Second Language Research, 33*(3), 325–40.

Guion, S., Flege, J., & Loftin, J. (2000). The effect of L1 use on pronunciation in Quicha- Spanish bilinguals. *Journal of Phonetics, 28,* 27–42.

Hammer, C., Komaroff, E., Rodriguez, B., Lopez, L., Scarpino, S., & Goldstein, B. (2012). Predicting Spanish-English bilingual children's language abilities. *Journal of Speech, Language, and Hearing Research, 55*(5), 1251–64.

Hartshorne, J., Tenenbaum, J., & Pinker, S. (2018). A critical period for second language acquisition: Evidence from 2/3 million English speakers. *Cognition, 177,* 263–77.

Herdina, P., & Jessner, U. (2013). The implications of language attrition for dynamic systems theory: Next steps and consequences. *International Journal of Bilingualism, 17*(6), 752–6.

Hernandez, A. E., & Kohnert, K. (1999). Aging and language switching in bilinguals. *Aging, Neuropsychology and Cognition, 6,* 69–83.

Hernandez, A. E., & Li, P. (2007). Age of acquisition: Its neural and computational mechanisms. *Psychological Bulletin, 133*(4), 638–50.

Hernandez, A. E., & Reyes, I. (2002). Within- and between-language priming differ: Evidence from repetition of pictures in Spanish-English bilinguals. *Journal of Experimental Psychology: Learning, Memory, and Cognition, 28,* 726–34.

Hernandez, A. E., Bates, E., & Avila, L. (1996). Processing across the language boundary: A cross-modal priming study of Spanish-English bilinguals. *Journal of Experimental Psychology: Learning, Memory and Cognition, 22,* 846–64.

Hernandez, A. E., Claussenius-Kalman, H., Ronderos, J., Castilla-Earls, A., Sun, L., Weiss, S., & Young, D. (2019a). Neuroemergentism: A framework for studying cognition and the brain. *Journal of Neurolinguistics*, *49*, 214–23.

Hernandez, A. E., Claussenius-Kalman, H., Ronderos, J., Castilla-Earls, A., Sun, L., Weiss, S., & Young, D. (2019b). Neuroemergentism: Response to commentaries. *Journal of Neurolinguistics*, *49*, 258–62.

Hernandez, A. E., Hofmann, J., & Kotz, S. (2007). Age of acquisition modulates neural activity for both regular and irregular syntactic functions. *Neuroimage*, *36*(3), 912–23.

Hernandez, A. E., Li, P., & MacWhinney, B. (2005). The emergence of competing modules in bilingualism. *Trends in Cognitive Science*, *9*, 220–5.

Hernandez, A. E. (2013). *The bilingual brain*. Oxford, England: Oxford University Press.

Jiang, B., & Kuehn, P. (2001). Transfer in the academic language development of post-secondary ESL students. *Bilingual Research Journal*, *25*, 417–36.

Johnson, J., & Newport, E. (1989). Critical period effects in second language learning: The influence of maturational state on the acquisition of English as a second language. *Cognitive Psychology*, *21*, 60–99.

Kartushina, N., Frauenfelder, U., & Golestani, N. (2016). How and when does the second language influence the production of native speech sounds: A literature review. *Language Learning*, *66*(S2), 155–86.

Kim, K., Relkin, N., Lee, K., & Hirsch, J. (1997). Distinct cortical areas associated with native and second languages. *Nature*, *388*(6638), 171–74.

Kohnert, K. (2004). Processing skills in early sequential bilinguals. In B. Goldstein (Ed.), *Bilingual Language Development and Disorders in Spanish-English Speakers* (pp. 53–76). Baltimore, MD: Brookes.

Kohnert, K. (2013). *Language Disorders in Bilingual Children and Adults* (2nd edn). San Diego, CA: Plural.

Köpke, B., & Schmid, M. (2003). Language attrition: The next phase. In M. Schmid, B. Köpke, M. Keijser, & L. Weilemar (Eds.), *First Language Attrition: The Next Phase; Proceedings of the International Conference on First Language Attrition: Interdisciplinary Perspectives on Methodological Issues*. Amsterdam, The Netherlands/Philadelphia, PA: Benjamins.

Köpke, B. (2004). Neurolinguistic aspects of attrition. *Journal of Neurolinguistics*, *17*, 3–30.

Krashen, S., Long, M., & Scarcella, R. (1979). Age, rate, and eventual attainment in second language acquisition. *TESOL Quarterly*, *9*, 573–82.

Kuo, L-J, Ramirez, G., de Marin, S., Kim, T-J, & Unal-Gezer, M. (2017). Bilingualism and morphological awareness: A study with children from general education and Spanish-English dual language programs. *Educational Psychology, 37*(2), 94–111.

Lahmann, C., Steinkrauss, R., & Schmid, M. (2016). Factors affecting grammatical and lexical complexity of long-term L2 speakers' oral proficiency *Language Learning, 66* (2), 354–85.

Li, P., Legault, J., & Litcofsky, K. (2014). Neuroplasticity as a function of second language learning: Anatomical changes in the human brain. *Cortex, 58*, 301–24.

Liu, H., & Cao, F. (2016). L1 and L2 processing in the bilingual brain: A meta-analysis of neuroimaging studies. *Brain and language, 159*, 60–73.

Long, M. (2013). Maturational constraints on child and adult SLA. In G. Granena & M. Long (Eds.), *Sensitive Periods, Language Aptitude, and Ultimate L2 Attainment* (pp. 3–41). Amsterdam, The Netherlands/ Philadelphia, PA: Benjamins.

Marian, V., Bartolotti, J., Rochanavibhata, S., Bradley, K., & Hernandez, A. E. (2017). Bilingual cortical control of between- and within-language competition. *Scientific Reports 7*, Article 1176.

Marian, V., Spivey, M., & Hirsch, J. (2003). Shared and separate systems in bilingual language processing: Converging evidence from eyetracking and brain imaging. *Brain and Language, 86*(1), 70–82.

Montrul, S. (1999). Causative errors with unaccusative verbs in L2 Spanish. *Second Language Research, 15*, 191–219.

Montrul, S. (2005). Second language acquisition and first language loss in adult early bilinguals: Exploring some differences and similarities. *Second Language Research, 21*, 199–249.

Montrul, S., Davidson, J., De La Fuente, I., & Foote, R. (2014). Early language experience facilitates the processing of gender agreement in Spanish heritage speakers. *Bilingualism: Language and Cognition, 17*(1), 118–38.

Newman, A., Tremblay, A., Nichols, E., Neville, H., & Ullman, M. (2012). The influence of language proficiency on lexical semantic processing in native and late learners of English. *Journal of cognitive neuroscience, 24*(5), 1205–23.

Nichols, E., & Joanisse, M. (2016). Functional activity and white matter microstructure reveal the independent effects of age of acquisition and proficiency on second-language learning. *NeuroImage, 143*, 15–25.

Nicoladis, E., Palmer, A., & Marentette, P. (2007). The role of type and token frequency in using past tense morphemes correctly. *Developmental Science, 10*, 237–54.

Nikolov, M. (Ed.) (2009). *Age Factor and Early Language Learning*. Berlin, Germany: De Gruyter.

Oyama, S. (1976). A sensitive period for the acquisition of a nonnative phonological system. *Journal of Psycholinguistic Research*, *5*, 261–85.

Pakulak, E., & Neville, H. (2011). Maturational constraints on the recruitment of early processes for syntactic processing. *Journal of Cognitive Neuroscience, 23*(10), 2752–65.

Pallier, C., Dehaene, S., Poline, J., LeBihan, D., Argenti, A., Dupoux, E., & Mehler, J. (2003). Brain imaging of language plasticity in adopted adults: Can a second language replace the first? *Cerebral Cortex*, *13*, 155–61.

Paradis, M. (1994). Neurolinguistic aspects of implicit and explicit memory: Implications for bilingualism and SLA. In N. Ellis (Ed.), *Implicit and Explicit Learning of Languages* (pp. 393–419). London: Academic Press.

Patterson, K., Lambon Ralph, M., Hodges, J., & McClelland, J. (2001). Deficits in irregular past-tense verb morphology associated with degraded semantic knowledge. *Neuropsychologia*, *39*, 709–24.

Perani, D., Paulesu, E., Galles, N., Dupoux., E., Dehaene, S., Bettinardi, V., ... Mehler, J. (1998). The bilingual brain: Proficiency and AOA in acquisition of a second language. *Brain*, *121*, 1841–52.

Plonsky, L., & Ghanbar, H. (2018). Multiple regression in L2 research: A methodological synthesis and guide to interpreting R2 values. *The Modern Language Journal*, *102*, 713–31.

Prior, A., Degani, T., Awawdy, S., Yassin, R., & Korem, N. (2017). Is susceptibility to cross-language interference domain specific? *Cognition*, *165*, 10–25.

Ramírez, J., Pasta, D., Yuen, S., Ramey, D., & Billings, D. (1991). Executive summary, Final report: *Longitudinal Study of Structured English Immersion Strategy, Early Exit and Late Exit Transitional Bilingual Programs for Language Minority Children*. San Mateo, CA: Aguirre International.

Raven, J., Raven, J., & Court, J. (1998). *Standard Progressive Matrices, 1998 Edition*. Oxford, England: Oxford Psychologists Press.

Rimfeld, K., Dale, P., & Plomin, R. (2015). How specific is second language-learning ability? A twin study exploring the contributions of first language achievement and intelligence to second language achievement. *Translational Psychiatry*, *5*, e638.

Rosmawati (2014). Second language developmental dynamics: How Dynamic Systems Theory accounts for issues in second language learning. *The Australian Educational and Developmental Psychologist*, *31(1)*, 66–80.

Rothman, J. (2008). Why all counter-evidence to the Critical Period Hypothesis in second language acquisition is not equal or problematic. *Language and Linguistics Compass*, *2*(6), 1063–88.

Sánchez, L. (2018). Epistemological issue with keynote article "The relevance of first language attrition to theories of bilingual development" by Monika S. Schmid and Barbara Köpke. In *Linguistic Approaches to Bilingualism, 7*(6), 754–8,

Schmid, M. (2014). The debate on maturational constraints in bilingual development: A perspective from first-language attrition. *Language Acquisition, 21*(4), 386–410.

Schmid, M., & Köpke, B. (2018a). The relevance of first language attrition to theories of bilingual development. *Linguistic Approaches to Bilingualism, 7*(6), 637–67.

Schmid, M., & Köpke, B. (2018b). When is a bilingual an attriter? *Linguistic Approaches to Bilingualism, 7*(6), 763–70.

Schmid, M., Köpke, B., & de Bot, K. (2013). Language attrition as a complex, non-linear development. *International Journal of Bilingualism, 17*(6) 675–82.

Silverberg, S., & Samuel, A. (2004). The effect of age of second language acquisition on the representation and processing of second language words. *Journal of Memory and Language, 51*, 381–98.

Stevens, G. (1999). Age at immigration and second language proficiency among foreign-born adults. *Language in Society, 28*, 555–78.

Stocco, A., Yamasaki, B., Natalenko, R., & Prat, C. (2014): Bilingual brain training: A neurobiological framework of how bilingual experience improves executive function. *International Journal of Bilingualism, 18*(1) 67–92

Thierry, G., & Wu, Y. (2007). Brain potentials reveal unconscious translation during foreign-language comprehension. *Proceedings of the National Academy of Sciences of the United States of America, 104*(30), 12530–35.

Tomasello, M. (2000). First steps toward a usage-based theory of language acquisition. *Cognitive Linguistics, 11*(1–2), 61–82.

Ullman, M. (1999). Acceptability ratings of irregular and regular past tense forms: Evidence for a dual system model of language from word frequency and phonological neighbourhood effects. *Language and Cognitive Process, 14*, 47–67.

Ullman, M. (2001). A neurocognitive perspective on language: The declarative/procedural model. *Nature Neuroscience, 2*, 717–26.

Valenzuela, A. (1999). *Subtractive Schooling: U.S.-Mexican Youth and the Politics of Caring*. Albany, NY: State University of New York Press.

van Boxtel, S., Bongaerts, T., & Coppen, P. (2003). Native-like attainment in L2 syntax. *EUROSLA Yearbook, 3*, 157–81.

Vaughn, K., & Hernandez, A. E. (2018). Becoming a balanced, proficient bilingual: Predictions from age of acquisition and genetic background. *Journal of Neurolinguistics*, *46*, 69–77.

Ventureyra, V., Pallier, C., & Yoo, H. (2004). The loss of first language phonetic perception in adopted Koreans. *Journal of Neurolinguistics*, *17*(1), 79–91.

Waldron, E., & Hernandez, A. E. (2013). The role of age of acquisition on past tense generation in Spanish-English bilinguals: An fMRI study. *Brain and Language*, *125*(1), 28–37.

Wartenberger, I., Heckeren, H., Abutalabi, J., Cappa, S., Villringer, A., & Perani, D. (2003). Early setting of grammatical processing in the bilingual brain. *Neuron*, *37*, 159–70.

Weber-Fox, C., & Neville, H. (1996). Maturational constraints on functional specialization for language processing: ERP and behavioral evidence in bilingual speakers. *Journal of Cognitive Neuroscience*, *8*, 231–56.

Weber-Fox, C., & Neville, H. (1999). Functional neural subsystems are differentially affected by delays in second language immersion: ERP and behavior evidence in bilinguals. In D. Birdsong (Ed.), *Second Language Acquisition and the Critical Period Hypothesis* (pp. 1–22), Mahwah, NJ: Erlbaum.

Wei, M., Joshi, A., Zhang, M., Mei, L., Manis, F., He, Q., . . . & Lu, Z.-L. (2015). How age of acquisition influences brain architecture in bilinguals. *Journal of Neurolinguistics*, *36*, 35–55.

Werker, J., & Hensch, T. (2015). Critical periods in speech perception: New directions. *Annual Review of Psychology*, *66*, 173–96.

White, L., & Genesee, F. (1996). How native is near-native? The issue of ultimate attainment in adult second-language acquisition. *Second Language Research*, *12*, 233–65.

Wong, B., Yin, B., & O'Brien, B. (2016). Neurolinguistics: Structure, function, and connectivity in the bilingual brain. *BioMed Research International*, Article 7069274.

Woodcock, R., & Munoz-Sandoval, A. (2001). *Woodcock-Munoz Language Survey: Normative Update*. Itasca, IL: Riverside.

Yeni-Komshian, G., Flege, J., & Liu, S. (2000). Pronunciation proficiency in the first and second languages of Korean-English bilinguals. *Bilingualism: Language and Cognition*, *3*, 131–49.

Zafar, S., & Meenakshi, K. (2012). Individual learner differences and second language acquisition: A review. *Journal of Language Teaching and Research*, *3*, 639–46.

Zou, L., Ding, G., Abutalebi, J., Shu, H., & Peng, D. (2012). Structural plasticity of the left caudate in bimodal bilinguals. *Cortex*, *48*(9), 1197–206.

Cambridge Elements ☰

Elements in Second Language Acquisition

Alessandro Benati

American University of Sharjah, UAE

Alessandro Benati is Professor of English and Applied Linguistics at the American University of Sharjah (UAE). He is internationally known for his research in second language acquisition and ground-breaking work on Processing Instruction. He has authored research monographs and articles in high-impact journals, including *Second Language Research* and *Language Teaching*. Alessandro is a member of AHRC Peer Review College, REF 2021, and honorary professor at the York St John University and the University of Portsmouth.

John W. Schwieter

Wilfrid Laurier University

John W. Schwieter is Associate Professor of Spanish and Linguistics and Faculty of Arts Teaching Scholar at Wilfrid Laurier University. His research interests include psycholinguistic and neurolinguistic approaches to multilingualism and language acquisition; second language teaching and learning; translation and cognition; and language, culture, and society.

About the Series

Second Language Acquisition showcases a high-quality set of updatable, concise works that address how learners come to internalize the linguistic system of another language and how they make use of that linguistic system. Contributions reflect the interdisciplinary nature of the field, drawing on theories, hypotheses, and frameworks from education, linguistics, psychology, and neurology, among other disciplines. Each Element in this series addresses several important questions: What are the key concepts? What are the main branches of research? What are the implications for SLA? What are the implications for pedagogy? What are the new avenues for research? What are the key readings?

Cambridge Elements ≡

Second Language Acquisition

Elements in the Series

Proficiency Predictors in Sequential Bilinguals: The Proficiency Puzzle
Lynette Austin, Arturo E. Hernandez, and John W. Schwieter

A full series listing is available at www.cambridge.org/esla

CPSIA information can be obtained
at www.ICGtesting.com
Printed in the USA
LVHW080855080419
613335LV00018B/179/P

9 781108 725248